SEX IS NOT TABOO

ISBN 978-976-95322-4-3

Printed by Northern Caribbean University Press
Manchester Road, Mandeville
Manchester, Jamaica, W.I.

Edited by
Marjorie Powis, Dip., Mass Comm.
Jessica Grant-Myers, BSc
Monica Grant, MA

Revised by
Lennoi Anderson

Cover Photos by Denieze Anderson
Design Layout by Garfield Forbes

Scriptures credited to the Holy Bible,
King James Version

ACKNOWLEDGEMENTS

Firstly, I must say thanks to the Almighty God
for life and His many blessings
afforded to me.
Then I must thank my wife who inspired me and made
Sex Is Not Taboo
possible.

I would also like to thank
Glendon Baker, Marjorie Powis, Lennoi Anderson, Garfield Forbes,
Monica Grant, Jessica Myers and Denieze Anderson
for the many hours spent putting
this book together and for being patient
with me as we went through the process.
I thank everyone from the bottom of my heart.
Without you all, I could not have done it.
Thank you!

L. E. Anderson
(876) 788-3282, (876) 454-3043
erolandy@yahoo.com

DEDICATION

This book is dedicated to my wife of over thirty years, Enid. Without her, this book would not have been possible. After getting married, I realized that misunderstandings are more common in marriage than understanding, patience needed more than impatience, and that where positive is needed negative is found.

With so much of what we were hoping for after all our years together, I have good reason to try to help others to be more positive in marriage. Some things that cause arguments make no sense. Divorce is all too common, and the world continues to do crazy things. But when one can turn negatives into positives, one hopes that others will learn from them.

The only real love is the love that never dies…

I also wish to dedicate this book to wives and husbands who are finding it difficult to live in peace and harmony, and to young people who are falling in love without knowing how to stay in love.

The ideas contained in this book are simple enough to help families put love into action, as God wills it, and to help make our world a better place. With God's help, all who read this book will become better lovers.

God's richest blessings upon you all!

FOREWORD

The title of this work, Sex Is Not Taboo, was very carefully selected by its author, Leonard Anderson. Though a man with very little formal schooling, he has very precise knowledge and a thorough understanding of what a relationship, as designed by our Creator, should be. For this reason, Leonard, an avid reader of a wide variety of books, not the least of which is the Bible, believes that the best sex education manual ever produced is the Holy Scriptures. He believes that the only way couples can live together in harmony is by following the instructions set out in the Bible, as opposed to living superficial lives.

Sex education, Anderson feels, should be taught from the pulpit, not 'swept under the carpet' by pastors who refuse to speak openly on the subject. Indeed, "Sex is not taboo," he says.

You are encouraged to keep turning the pages of this book wherein you will find some plain, practical and simple solutions to the problems that face families today. There are also valuable insights to help young people understand that sex is a gift from God, given to us for recreation and procreation, within the context of marriage, which, if handled according to His will, is very fulfilling and helps to make life complete.

There is advice for married individuals who, as the author says, are often some of the loneliest people in the world, who contribute to the "dead" state of some congregations. "Stop lying about the 'sexless' state of your relationships!" he tells married couples. "Face it for what it is, and deal with it!"

Keep reading!

Marjorie Powis
(Journalist/Public Relations/Marketing Practitioner)

Leonard Anderson is a man who is passionate in his view that relationships should be Christ-centered. This book is an insight into the profound intellect that has carved out the time to engage others in a subject that is so common yet which has left such a trail of disappointment, unease, and downright destruction in its wake.

Sex Is Not Taboo should be required reading for anyone who is thinking of starting a relationship, in a new relationship, or been in a relationship for years.

As it says in the book, "The mind is not something that you can see, yet one can read the mind." Read the book and see the things you never thought possible in relationships.

Glendon Baker
(Radio Broadcaster)

The information contained in this volume entitled Sex Is Not Taboo is designed to help partners who are in or out of crisis to experience sexual bliss as God intended it to be. It should serve as a manual for the sexually ignorant and a refresher for those who may have fallen by the way.

It is the author's intention that the insights presented within these pages will serve their desired purpose, and for the information to be shared.

Monica Grant (Teacher), **Jessica Grant-Myers** (Editor)

Sex! How exactly did something originally meant for holiness earn such a dirty reputation? Why has something so beautiful, even the means to the creation of lives we value so much – especially our own – become this monster of a taboo? Somewhere along the line, something went terribly wrong.

Sex, as we know it today, is but a shadow of what Adam and Eve first experienced in the garden. After God performed that first marriage ceremony, can you imagine the excitement they must have felt in getting to 'know' each other! Sure, sin eventually came into the picture, but when you have known a great thing you do not shut up about it. Word spreads… Imperfect though it had become, I would like to believe they knew how to talk openly and candidly with their children, grandchildren and great-grandchildren about the joys to be had in a union as beautiful as theirs. Unfortunately, their descendants (you and I) further marred by sin, have lost their innocence.

As it was in the days of Noah, so it is today: marriage upon marriage, the endless yet empty pursuit of happiness… We obviously all want what our first parents had. Yet with the way things are now, continuously degraded since the fall, we keep going about it in the wrong way. We all want the spouse, the sex, the children, the "dream," but that element which keeps it all together is sorely missing: LOVE. The God of love is needed now, perhaps more than ever, to heal today's shadows of what family ought to be.

My father recognizes the plight of the modern family. At the heart of this plight he sees a MONSTER three-letter word that needs a re-introduction. Sex has fallen far through the years, from an expression of love to an outlet for lust. The family union is broken because its very unifying foundation is shaken. Sex! How can it be taboo when it is the key to opening the doors to better, healthier family relationships?

Lennoi Anderson
(Musician)

CONTENTS

1.	God And Sex	1
2.	Saving Your Family	2
3.	Equality And Humility In Marriage	4
4.	Pastoral Silence	6
5.	No Shame In Not Knowing	8
6.	Waiting For Sex	10
7.	Communication: The Best Romance	12
8.	The One Look Method	14
9.	Caught In The Act	16
10.	Wanting A Man	18
11.	Knowing What You Want	20
12.	Locking Your Bedroom Door	22
13.	Remembering Your Children	24
14.	Intimacy, Insemination And God's Love	26
15.	Good Sex In Marriage	29
16.	The Evils Of Money	32
17.	Your Best Counselor	35
18.	Selfishness And Poverty	37
19.	The World In One Person	39
20.	Divorce	41
21.	The Lord's Heritage	43
22.	Sexual Frequency	45
23.	Granting Favors	47
24.	Speaking Of Sex...	49
25.	No Holding Back	51
26.	Who Is The Greatest?	53
27.	Hope For Mismatched Couples	55
28.	Whatever It Takes	57
29.	Getting Satan Out	58
30.	A Disease Called Loneliness	61
31.	Why Sex Is Taboo For Some	63
32.	Shallow Love	64
33.	Rejection	65
34.	Standard	66
35.	Energy	69
36.	Length Of Life	71
37.	Maintaining Your Marriage	72
38.	Waiting For The Other World	73
39.	Deception	74

40.	Excitement	75
41.	Wedding Trash	76
42.	Taking Care Of Your Yard	77
43.	Who Is Your Hero?	78
44.	As A Man	79
45.	A Useless Devil	81
46.	Stimulating The Mind	82
47.	The Hidden Man/Woman	84
Endnotes, Part One: Secrets To A Happy Marriage		86
Endnotes, Part Two: Love Simplified		88
Doing What Seems Impossible		Inside Back Cover
About The Author		Back Cover

CHAPTER 1

GOD AND SEX

One of God's greatest acts of love was in giving us the gift of sex for our creative pleasure. Sex is an extraordinary endowment that should be thoroughly enjoyed by all married couples. Within the framework of marriage, sex enhances not just your love life, but also your life of love for others, your Christianity, and is a foretaste of the joys of salvation in the heavenly kingdom. God has a deep concern for marriages, especially those professing Christianity. God did not cause man and woman to be ashamed of their bodies… Our timidity was, and still is, the result of sin.

CHAPTER 2

SAVING YOUR FAMILY

nyone contemplating marriage should only do so for the right reasons, because marriage is a God-given responsibility that no one should take lightly. It was instituted in the Garden of Eden, as God saw that it was not good for the man, Adam, to be alone. Now, this being the case, why then do so many of us take so lightly such an important union as the family? We ought to feel honored to be a part of a family and, as such, willingly co-operate with the head of the home, always remembering there is a Supreme head, Jesus Christ. For God is not the author of confusion.

Remember, there is a heaven to gain. Contentious and undisciplined families will not be there; joyful and unselfish families will be there, for Jesus Himself will be there too. As for myself, I certainly want to be there! I do not know of anything on earth that is sweeter to me than seeing my family living peaceably with each other. The joy it gives is overwhelming! And that is why, as I move about meeting people, I encourage them to foster harmonious relationships with each other, every chance I get. The rewards will be great even in our temporal lives, since most things naturally improve when a person is happy and has a peaceful state of mind – even if you have a bad heart, it will most likely not attack when you are happy.

Far too often we 'murder' our loved ones by doing and saying unkind things to and about them, things yielding unhappiness. We need to stop… and do the opposite. Treat people with kindness and respect while they are alive, and do not wait until they die to start crying 'crocodile tears' of love, as some of us who are mere pretenders are likely to do. It is all about small gestures, like being prepared for an honest answer when we ask someone,

"Whatever we may do with it, it will never be true love until we demonstrate it."

"How are you?" We tend to expect a positive response, but what if the answer is not what we expected? What if the person answers by saying, "I'm hungry, but I don't have any money to buy food"? What do we do then?

Be genuine. Show sincere interest: "What can I do for you?" "Can I be of any help today?" "What's going on in your life?" … If you really love someone, do not forget to say as often as possible, "I love you."

I often wonder how many people on earth truly know how powerful that four-letter word "LOVE" is. I believe it is the most popular word in the world, but the least meant or understood. We say it, but we hate it. We sing it, but we hate it. We play it, but we hate it. We dance it, but we hate it. We write it, but we hate it. We email it, but we hate it. Whatever we may do with it, it will never be true love until we demonstrate it. By simple demonstrations of love, we may create a little heaven in our homes.

CHAPTER 3

EQUALITY AND HUMILITY IN MARRIAGE

There are couples out there that are not real. That is, their relationships are one-sided. There are husbands who think themselves better than their wives. Sounds strange? I wish it were, but it is a real scenario in a very real world. When things are going great, some men allow pride to step in and allow other women to come into the picture, women whom they eventually see as more beautiful than their wives. All this is part of the devil's deception.

Husbands and wives are equals. They may often not act as such, but truth remains. That is why wives and husbands must behave like true sweethearts. Sweethearts are sexy, outgoing, loving, kind, reliable, thankful, respectful, virtuous… A one-sided relationship is no good, and no woman or man should ever be in one. Life is too short to let it waste away in unfulfillment. Ladies, strive to outdo him in acts of love and kindness; and gentlemen, strive to outdo her. Where there is equity, there is harmony.

Man and woman complete each other. A man cannot give birth, but he is a part of the process of creating new life; a woman can give birth, but she would have nothing to birth were it not for a man. How can we solve the problem of inequality that we have created for ourselves? Stop being foolish, and respect one another. Make everyday sweeter than the day before, and do not wait until you lose your money and your good looks (or maybe even a hand, a foot, an eye, or a breast) to realize how blessed you are. Without good memories of your lives together, what will keep that wife or husband from straying?

> ## *"A man cannot give birth, but he is a part of the process of creating new life; a woman can give birth, but she would have nothing to birth were it not for a man."*

Observe some elderly people and you can tell they were physically beautiful in their youth. Some of them were possibly proud. Now they are humble. There is a lesson in this for us all: Do not wait until you are old to practice humility. Respect is due to your spouse. She is not a helper; he is not a yard-boy. He is your husband; she is your wife. Remember, sex is not taboo! Enjoy it while you can, for the night comes when no man or woman can work. By then, it will be the memories, the memories... According to one man, you might just have to clap and rub. Who knows?

CHAPTER 4

PÁSTORÁL SILENCE

We live in world where sex is taboo, even within the realm of Christianity. Pastors should therefore not hesitate to address the subject from the pulpit. They should talk about love and romance as straightforwardly as possible. Why? Pastors are persons whom the general public looks up to. As such, if they were to preach or educate more openly on the subject at hand, less young people would be lead astray by worldly influence.

I would hope that pastors not view these statements as an attack, though observations are often thus misconstrued. But when a pastor says something, people are more likely to believe it. We should recognize the great influence pastors have on their congregations, especially regarding this topic that is as real as life, as real as food, as real as taking a shower, as real as reality. Without sex, none of us would be here! God chose sex as the means through which earth would be kept vibrant and full of life until He returns. But sin has made a mockery of every wonderful and good thing that God has made. We must put a stop to it, and pastors have one of the biggest platforms from which to make a difference.

I have been attending church for over half a century, and have been listening for practical sermons on the topic, but what I hear mostly are preachers beating around the bush. Encouraging people to get married for the sake of not living common law 'sweetheart' lives is just not good enough. Married couples must be taught how to treat each other. It takes everything to make a marriage work. Yet some things are more important than others, and the one we are most afraid to talk about is the one that is most important. There are couples that act as though sex is never a problem in their relationship. Instead, they might tell you, "I didn't cook his dinner… I didn't iron his shirt… I didn't have any money…" Nonsense! Their troubles are in the bedroom, but they downright refuse to talk about it.

Common sense dictates that if romance, love and affection remain at their peak in the relationship, as they should, couples would fare much bet-

*"...what I hear
mostly are
preachers beating around
the bush."*

ter. And we wonder why our congregations are so dead! Think about how many lonely people sit in front of you, dear Pastor. Indeed, some Christian married folks are among the loneliest people in the world. If marriages happened for the right reasons and the relationships were maintained, things would be far different. The divorce rate would certainly not be so high.

A brother of mine once said, "If there's anything in the world nicer than a woman, I'd like to see it," to which I replied, "If there's anything nicer than a woman, I don't want to see it." You see, whichever way you put it, you are going to reach the same conclusion: Women are just too wonderful to put things above. I wish both genders would see each other in the same light, each highly esteeming the other. The best gift you can give your children is that of mother and father living together in harmony. It is with this in mind that I call upon pastors to do more for families by speaking openly and honestly about sex.

CHAPTER 5

NO SHAME IN NOT KNOWING

What one does not know, one should not be ashamed of. Every relationship has a beginning. Once you have a beginning, a learning process also begins. If both are willing to learn, that is a good thing; if both are not willing to learn, the relationship is dead before it even begins – if one is willing and the other is not, get out of it!

What makes love 'real' is when two people from different backgrounds come together and make the necessary adjustments to ensure each other's happiness. A person who finds someone who 'fits' his or her lifestyle, thinking they have found love, is making a huge mistake. The person may suit your lifestyle, and it undoubtedly feels good, but that is not love. You risk being like a pair of old shoes – you wear it because it is comfortable, though it is not the best. The better shoes are not as comfortable at first, but they are quality, so you wear them until they get comfortable. That is love.

Jesus left heaven, came to earth, and suffered 'change' so we could be saved. Now THAT is love! You cannot change anyone, but you should be willing to change your [bad] habits in order to accommodate the person you hope to be with. There are those who say it does not matter, as long as it fits or feels good. But this is not good enough. You must stand for something, or you will fall for anything. Genuine love is what we should all strive for. A false perception of love will destroy romance and make sex feel like torture. Never get complacent; there is always room for improvement. If we are really in love – if we want love to work –, we must be willing to learn.

The Bible plainly says we should be married before engaging in sex, and most Christians agree. The question is, ow will you know what to do? Two virgins get married and they are in love, but they do not want to learn from each other – what do you think will happen? Their marriage could be

"If both are not willing to learn,
the relationship is dead
before it even begins..."

over in record time. This is why you must be willing to learn from each other. Marriage is an adventure, meaning you do not know where you are going, but you should allow love to take you there.

Journeying together can be great fun, but fussing and quarreling with each other will surely take that fun away. Consequently, conversation is an essential skill worthy of mastery. Your spouse should be your best friend, lawyer, doctor, psychologist, teacher – your everything! Do not allow your spouse to feel inferior by turning to everyone but him or her. Rather, build a supportive relationship with each other, yet not in wrongdoing.

King Ahab and his wife Jezebel, Ananias and his wife Sapphira – they were living together in one accord, but they were selfish. As a result, they were destroyed. Life is great, but it is greater when we live it for each other, in selfless love. If you do not give love, you will not receive love – though if you keep it, it has no value. Love is a shared experience exemplified in marriage, wherein the two become one flesh.

To fight with your spouse, then, is to fight with yourself. How foolish to fight with oneself! If you do not wish to learn, then do not live with anyone, especially in a romantic situation. In relationships, doing your own thing is unacceptable – "Do unto others as you would have them do unto you" (Matthew 7:12). To fight with your spouse is to fight a losing battle. Selfishness might seem to work sometimes, but only for a while. Be unselfish. Make learning a part of your life, and, as you learn, impart. Mutual unselfishness guarantees your togetherness will be one of happiness, joy, laughter and peace.

CHAPTER 6

Sex was created by God and given to man for the purposes of pleasure and procreation. Strict guidelines were also given that man should not indulge in sex outside of marriage. But with the entrance of sin into the world, all hell broke loose!

People are having sex left, right and center, albeit under cover (pun intended), yet somehow it is taboo to openly talk about it. According to God's plan, the best thing to do is WAIT. Unfortunately, it hardly ever plays out that way. With peer pressure and the evil one at work, hormones going crazy, limited examples of self-control, movies and television programs screaming sex, Sex, SEX, only a Christ-like lifestyle can hold it back.

Evidently, one of society's chief problems is the shortage of healthy, parental sexual role modeling. In fact, parents should really be positive trendsetters for their children in all things, not just the sexual. Sadly, though, the breakdown in families is so bad that young people see no need for waiting to have sex.

With husbands and wives at war, sweethearts burning the house down when their relationship turns sour, lovers cursing and hurting one another so much, what is there to encourage young people to wait, let alone hope for a happy coupling in marriage?

In waiting, only "with Christ in the vessel can we smile at the storm." Christian couples, the very ones who should be shining examples of good marriage relations, need to do better. Much of what children learn is not learnt from parents, because parents are often too ashamed to talk about sexual matters. But as parents, we should be prepared to tell our young people how interesting and wonderful sex is…and why they should wait.

If parents act like sex is a painful chore, their children will have confused questions in their minds – "If sex is so bad, why do I feel so good

> ## *"With…hormones going crazy, limited examples of self-control, movies and television programs screaming sex, Sex, SEX, only a Christ-like lifestyle can hold it back."*

when she holds my hand?" Parents must be honest about sex and more flexible in discussing matters that are important to their children. They do not want to hear one thing and see their parents' lives saying something else. Better to live what we preach and preach what we live.

If our relationship with each other as parents is dysfunctional, it gives young ones the idea that it makes no sense to marry only to end up fussing and fighting. Let us give peace in our homes a chance, so the family will return to its rightful place in the world. Only then will young people understand the true importance of waiting until marriage to have sex.

CHAPTER 7

COMMUNICATION: THE BEST ROMANCE

Ever since sin entered the world, there has been a breakdown in communication with God and one another. Regrettably, this has caused us a lot of grief. Humans were designed to communicate intelligently in order to make their lives easier. Good communication is a hallmark of good living, and the converse is true of bad communication – why then not choose the good? The evil one is always seeking to destroy anything that is good, and one of the methods he uses is confusion.

Satan learned firsthand of confusion's effectiveness. Remember the Tower of Babel? God had to confuse the language of the people who were building it in order to stop them from going any further with their project. We are no different from the Nimrod crew: If our communication with our spouses, colleagues at the work place, extended family members or friends is poor, we are in serious trouble. If we communicate well, on the other hand, many positive things will happen in our lives.

Yet because there tends to be so much negativity in the world, we often complain about how sinful it is, perhaps even blame the devil for a few of our mishaps – and he is guilty. But since we know he is around, we must try our best to keep him out of our business and keep the lines of positive communication open.

At the funeral service of the late Hugh Lawson Shearer, Edward Seaga in paying tribute noted that he had a good rapport with Shearer. Once during an overseas trip, something went awry in Jamaica and Shearer had called to update him on the situation. He recounted that all Shearer had to say was, "Mmhm, mmhm, mmhm," and the message was understood.

Now, if politicians can have such an understanding, we too can make good communication the hallmark of your lives together. Healthy commu-

> ## *"Humans were designed to communicate intelligently in order to make their lives easier."*

nication takes the taboo out of sex. It drives away fear, gives energy and keeps away hypertension, reducing the possibility of a heart attack. Great communication lightens your burdens, teaches unselfishness, allows you to pray together always, and keeps you in love…forever.

Is that not what it is all about – forever? If love is not a part of the business of living, life is worthless. If you hope to really live, love without reservation. Love is lovely, whether you partake of it or not, so you might as well get in on the action and make love happen.

CHAPTER 8

So often we say we are in love, yet we do not really know our spouses. We merely think we know that man or woman whom we are with. Our ignorance is our bliss, and it suggests that we are not as smart as we would like to think we are – we have no idea how 'unsmart' we are. Truth is, when couples know each other, all it takes is one look. It is often said that a picture is worth a thousand words; but in the case of loving husbands and wives, all it takes is one look shared between them. One look across the room can mean "It's time to go, honey," "Five more minutes," "I'm starving," or "I'm ready like Freddy, baby!"

Understanding each other's secret codes of communication certainly deepens the shared bond of intimacy. Sharing a wink, mouthing an "I love you" across the aisle, or stealing a kiss here and there, can help keep the fire burning. Calling during the day and saying something meant for his or her ears only could mean the difference between a hot night and a cold shower.

Even the simplest of gestures are bound, in their own way, to ease possible tension at work, put a smile on his or her face and make him or her eager to get home…to be with YOU. It means you understand each other: You are "in love!" It puts more spontaneity and fun into your love life, as your own happiness is bound up with the happiness of the one you

> ### *'One look across the room*
> ### *can mean "It's time to go, honey,"*
> ### *"Five more minutes,"*
> ### *"I'm starving,"*
> ### *or*
> ### *"I'm ready like Freddy, baby!"'*

are with – The Golden Rule…

It is especially the little things that enliven the spirit, stimulate the mind and put the body in the right frame of being. Some people say and believe with all their heart that they are romantic, yet they have no clue that one of the best ways to acknowledge love is to take that one look... Learn to look your spouse in the eye. Work on that 'look', and make your shared life together the best it can be.

CHAPTER 9

The scenario of the woman caught in adultery (John 8:1-11) is a perfect example of the typical Christian attitude towards sexuality. Persons who are openly romantic or even the slightest bit sexual are usually regarded as lewd and outrageous, and it is even worse for prostitutes. But thank God for Jesus who understands this aspect of our humanity – He should, after all, for He created it! That is the reason He so gently forgave her sins, she who in the eyes of everyone else was nothing more than a common whore. An attitude of hypocrisy cannot be hid from Christ, for the men who wanted her stoned were churchgoers, though they themselves endorsed adultery in not also presenting the guilty man before Jesus for judgment.

Men throughout history have looked down on prostitutes, in spite of the fact that many of them – though they will not readily admit this – would not know whether they are real men if it were not for the prostitute. You see, the women who are supposed to be like prostitutes [in their bedrooms] are not doing so. Sex is taboo for them: they cover themselves up, and take their men for granted. So the devil provides the 'ladies of the night' to fill the gap for "whosoever will come."

For this simple reason, prostitutes will always be in business. When you and I invite people to accept Christ, especially sexually active young people, what do we say to them when they do not see married couples leading by example – examples of Christians living romantic, passionate lives? We Christians must be mindful of what we display to the world, because the world is already confused. Now is not the time to hold back from your spouse: it is time to let go. A prostitute may not love whom she goes to bed with, but chances are that she loves her work.

> *"...many of them – though they will not readily admit this – would not know whether they are real men if it were not for the prostitute."*

Personally, I have a great deal of respect for them, because I believe prostitutes are among the most honest women in the world. Some may not love what they do, but they do their part, unlike some Christians who are living a lie. We bear the titles of husband and wife, yet we are far from fulfilling our roles.

CHAPTER 10

Reasoning with unmarried women over the years, I have always marveled at the things they say: "All good men are married," "Nuh good man nuh deh again," "Di man dem a ginnal," "Di man dem too selfish." And all conclude, "When I find a good man, I'm going to do everything to make him happy."

These comments are interesting... Though every woman makes the claim of knowing how to make her man happy, many married men with whom I have spoken claim that they are starved for love and affection from their wives. Is it a case of "wanty-wanty nuh get it – getty-getty nuh want it"? We are talking about marriage here, so I would hope not. There are still many good men available for women in search of Mr. Right. As such, a woman ought to prepare for her Mr. Right by becoming a Ms. Right.

We want everything, but expect to give nothing in return. There is a word for that: Selfishness. The devil has been selfish since the beginning of his downfall and is even more selfish today, because he has yet more hearts to turn from God. Therefore, if you want to keep the man you hope to find, keep the devil out of your heart, and keep your eyes on the prize. Forget what you do not have, remember what you need, and you will become Mrs. Right.

Samson was physically the strongest man mentioned in the Bible, yet he ranked among the weakest of men in his passion for Delilah. She was a cunning woman who knew how to use her feminine wiles to charm a man,

> ## *"If you want to keep the man*
> ## *you hope to find,*
> ## *keep the devil out of your heart,*
> ## *and keep your eyes*
> ## *on the prize."*

the result being her deceiving Sampson into revealing the secret of his physical strength. Women, you need not become tricksters like Delilah, though it would yield honest results if you use her methods honestly.

A man likes to feel a woman's affection, which complements communication. If you really love him, tell him. Do not keep it bottled up inside. Humans cannot read minds. Delilah manipulated Sampson for evil purposes. As a Christian woman, use your persuasive powers to get the best out of your man. In this way, you help him to remain Mr. Right.

Relationships are like a delicate plant: If you put it in the soil and leave it to fend for itself, it will wither and die. They are also like a newly built house and get rundown rather quickly if not maintained. Finding Mr. Right is one thing, but keeping him is another. It is up to you.

KNOWING WHAT YOU WANT

We are living in a world full of confusion. This confusion persists not for lack of a guide, but because we fail to acknowledge, believe and follow that guide: The Bible. Christians, however, need not be confused. We ought to know better. Do we not know that it is the evil one who has sown the seed of discord? The sooner we set our priorities right, the better off we shall be.

Life can be really simple:

- "Fear God and keep His commandments, for this is the whole duty of man" (Ecclesiastes 12:13).
- Love and respect your family.
- Love everyone. Give all the love you can, while you can, to all you can.
- "Do unto others as you would have them do unto you" (Matthew 7:12).

Your priorities should be ordered in such a way that you enrich the lives of others, which will in turn enrich your own life. Remember Solomon? Although he could have asked for ANYTHING he desired, all that he asked for was the wisdom to lead his people. He received what he had asked for and much more. He became the world's richest, in both wisdom and material wealth. Likewise, we must be wise enough to never allow material goods to be our top priority, lest we end up with little or nothing. Instead, let all your pursuits, especially that of a life partner, be motivated by love.

> ## *"The energy fueled by the desire to love is more than is gained from any nourishing food."*

The energy fueled by the desire to love is more than is gained from any nourishing food. When you eat too much, you feel sluggish; but no one can ever love too much, for the love of God is empowering!

If everyone's first priority were to love, can you imagine what the world would be like? The earth made new will have its foundation upon this very principle. If you and I wish to be a part of it, we had better start loving! If you do not know how, start by asking someone, like your husband or wife, what love is. Or better yet, ask God, the Author of Love.

Everybody wants to be loved, though only a few actually give love. If you are married and want to remain happily married, your marriage should be your first priority. This mindset would certainly eliminate many of the problems affecting society today.

CHAPTER 12

LOCKING YOUR BEDROOM DOOR

Privacy is something everyone is entitled to, especially adults. Sadly, though, parents seldom get any privacy, on account of their children. While they are undoubtedly cute and cuddly, children are among the most selfish of persons, they just do not know it. So what can a couple to do?

Think of your bedroom as being the most private area in your home. Keep its door(s) locked one hundred percent of the time. Sounds harsh? Well, maybe a little. But here is why: Parents must leave no room for ambiguity. If children grow up knowing that they are not allowed in their parents' bedroom, they will come to respect that space as their parents' private sanctuary. This way, when parents desire to spend a few private moments together (whether for intimacy or other business), there will be no doubt in their children's minds that "mommy and daddy need some time to themselves."

Having to calculate your children's whereabouts for the sake of 'stealing' a few loving moments together is bad practice. A friend of mine once said that whenever she and her husband wanted "to do anything" they had to send their daughter, a seven-year-old, next door to the neighbor's. This situation may have inconvenienced the neighbor, as well. Consequently, if you want your marriage to be as liberal as it was in the beginning, take the steps necessary to keep it that way. And keep your bedroom door shut at all times!

A "Knock Before You Enter" rule will not hurt anyone. Never allow your children to put out the fire of your love life, for you are going to need the passion long after the children are gone. So what if they have their little 'suspicions' about what you are doing behind closed doors! You are the adults, and you are in charge. Besides, after a while, they will not even care. Always reserve some private time for you and your spouse. Far too many couples reduce their lovemaking to those tired moments in the midnight hours when the children are asleep. Do not let your children control

> ## *"Having to calculate your children's whereabouts for the sake of 'stealing' a few loving moments together is bad practice."*

your love life like that! Let them grow up with the awareness that it is natural and healthy for parents to share private moments together.

Avoid those nights where you are both dead-tired and the episode ends up being nothing more than a 'slam-bam-thank-you-ma'am' followed immediately by snoring. Such a routine can get monotonous and extremely boring. Sure, you can go away on weekends to have some privacy, but how often can you afford a weekend getaway? Make your bedroom as private as that hotel room you cannot afford as often as you would like.

In privacy you will find the perfect opportunity to enrich your lives together, especially during the energy of youth. Enjoy experiencing all you can together. Enjoy the scent and taste of everything you can together. Enjoy eating and laughing together…

Simply enjoy each other's company!

CHAPTER 13

REMEMBERING YOUR CHILDREN

Marriage is a total package involving every aspect of life. Someone is invariably affected by everything you do and not do, so it is essential for both parties to consider the implications of their actions, especially when children are involved.

The nurturing of children is one of the greatest tasks a couple could ever undertake. Your spouse, however, should be your top priority and foremost responsibility. In many marriages, the children come first and the needs of the children are placed above the needs of each other. This ought not to be so. Were you not together before the children came along? It is your spouse with whom you fell in love and became "one flesh" (Genesis 2:24); thus if you stay in love, your children will get the best love that both of you can give. They need both parents, because children do indeed live what they learn.

When a daughter grows up seeing her mother treating her father with love and respect, she will do the same for her husband. Similarly, the son will do the same for his wife, based on his father's treatment of his mother. The home is undeniably the ultimate training ground for our children – as the saying goes, 'Good families make good communities, and good communities make good nations.'

I have often heard parents say, "Mi nuh business 'bout [him/her] any-

> *"In many marriages,*
> *the children come first*
> *and the needs of the children*
> *are placed above the needs of each other.*
> *This ought not to be so."*

more… All mi care 'bout a mi children!" But no one person makes a child – the children belong to both of you. Maybe if the term 'our' children is used, as opposed to 'my' children, there would be a reversal in the breakdown of the family relationship. Do not fight each other for the affections of your children. They were created by God and given to you both as a gift. Treat them as though they are yours equally.

CHAPTER 14

INTIMACY, INSEMINATION AND GOD'S LOVE

A couple's lifestyle should be worthy of emulation, though many couples fall short of attaining this ideal. Some couples, typically their female half, walk half-naked on the streets, creating opportunity for onlookers to lust. In such instances, conscientious couples may recognize the importance of keeping their love life at home so engaging that neither party will feel the need to encourage or entertain lustful feelings in others. Modesty is always tasteful, whether you have someone to go home to or not.

There is much temptation beyond the confines of home. Let husbands and wives not push each other aside, unconcerned with the powerful influence of the world. Each must acknowledge their attraction towards the opposite sex and be ready to fulfill that desire in each other.

For lack of passionate fulfillment at home, married men and women are seriously affected by what they see on the streets – after all, if you had no 'nature' you would not get that 'urge'. Marriage is not just about cooking and cleaning and other such things, for you can easily pay to get your laundry done, or buy lunch and order dinner; marriage is about total companionship coupled with open exploration of the sexual aspect of our design. God could have simply populated the world Himself, but He did not. Just as children are born of people in love, so He desires that our service to Him be the byproduct of love.

No better illustration of the depth of God's love for mankind is there than that most profound connection shared by a husband and wife during sexual intercourse. This is the crux of the matter and what intimacy is all about! But in these modern times where insemination can be performed

> ## *"Marriage is about total companionship coupled with open exploration of the sexual aspect of our design."*

without the intimate act God had intended, even without copulation, the bonds of intimacy between God and us have been weakened or broken.

All must strive to understand more deeply, Christians in particular, the inseparable connection between God, love and sex, lest we continue to behave erratically about things intimate and erotic. We need increased awareness of all such matters, and should thereby reflect it in our Christian lives. As Christians, we ought to have a better understanding of life issues in general than those of other socio-spiritual persuasions.

The world at large refuses to reflect upon the deeper consequences of her actions, and that is why so many live a life full of contradictions. If perchance you were to venture into some of the homes of the very persons who walk the streets scantily clad, you would be surprised to find them fully clothed, because they want nothing to do with their husbands or wives. Even this is a symptom of evil forces at work attempting to overrule God's design. When Satan has influence over our minds, it breeds negative thoughts about who we are with, thoughts of being married too long to someone not as pretty or handsome as others we might have had or could yet have. And so we see a reflection of the minds of individuals in the clothes they choose to wear in public, the advertisement of their sexuality being a sign of a lingering void that neither fooling around nor fornication can fill. And still preachers dwell upon the problem of illicit sexual behavior, without prescribing viable solutions or ways of remaining true to oneself and commitments!

Discussions on intimacy fit perfectly within the church setting, for Christ likens His church unto a woman, His bride, and He is her Husband. Women are very important, and they need to recognize who they really are. Men also need to recognize themselves. Both sexes must know their worth and feel validated with or without the world's appreciation. If you, whether man or woman, are starved for the world's attention, it does not bode well for your character, because the approval you receive from your spouse should be more highly prized than the world's. All the same, if you want the world's admiration so badly, remain unmarried. Correspondingly, in following Jesus, one must forsake everything else. It all comes right back to the Christ-Husband/Church-bride comparison and the importance of intimacy.

Where is the intimacy in moving from woman to woman or man to man? A prostitute loves no one; she belongs to whoever can afford her in the moment. When you love someone, your love is exclusive and without price – you just cannot get enough! It is the same way with the word of God. I read the Bible and laugh all the time, because it is true and perfect, sweet and powerful. When love is as love should be, it is just as wholesome as God's word. God certainly would not have given us something to enjoy unless it were perfectly good.

Subsequently, the solution to the 'sex in the streets' problem is a simple idea: good relations at home between husbands and wives. With something wonderful waiting for them at home, men and women are less likely to become victims of society's shameless attempts at seduction. Many times, however, the person waiting at home is not the attractive individual whom they had married, so lovers stray even without conscious thought. Recognize that your partner has eyes that see and a heart that feels, and be wise enough to stay connected in every way that matters.

Is there anything more pleasurable and beautiful than being joined with the naked body of the one you love? Beyond copulation itself, a naked body is a feast for the eyes. Is the home not the territory of man and wife, their Garden of Eden? As Adam and Eve were naked and not ashamed, in this fashion may a modern couple be within their own kingdom, physically and emotionally. Sure, leave something to the imagination from time to time – a little mystery goes a long way in making the thoughts run wild. Learn to mix things up, celebrate being together, and show mutual appreciation. That is what it is all about.

CHAPTER 15

GOOD SEX IN MARRIAGE

After getting married, some people undergo a shift in their attitude, and it is not always for the better. The devil is ever at work attempting to destroy everything we build, especially our marriages. As he worms his way into our relationships, it is impossible to have good sex because of the unpleasant atmosphere created by his influence. The wrong attitude is definitely a turn off, since the mind itself is a sex organ. While some may imagine themselves to be so sexy that just the sight of their naked body is enough to turn anyone on, it is not necessarily so. Sometimes ATTITUDE is everything!

The way you carry yourself, the way you are, and the way you relate with your partner gets etched into their memory. It is often what you remember that will turn you on or off. A man could be right next to his woman yet not 'see' her at all, even when she is naked, as all he sees is a cloud of misery surrounding her. Memories of a quarrel can just as easily haunt you. A favor undone or requests denied are all seeds the enemy can sow to a couple's detriment. Once they take root, sex will no longer be fulfilling; copulation may take place, but it feels more like rape.

When you are with someone, you are supposed to be reflecting on how wonderful they are, their beautiful character and the sweet things they do. Instead, many find themselves thinking the opposite and fooling themselves that such is the way of married life, "teeth and tongue will meet" – the only time teeth and tongue should meet is when kissing! Quarrels can be kept civil or to a minimum by reminding each other that dissension is the devil's ploy, his way of destroying beautiful things. Sometimes you have to surrender and recognize that your partner is worth pleasing. Or better yet, come to a reasonable compromise.

Placing your partner at the top of your priorities and list of people to

"Let your marriage be an opportunity for furthering your education in opening your heart to God's love through the opening of your life to another person."

please is simple, once you acknowledge that you are not perfect and expect to be equally valued by your partner. Nobody is perfect, and thus humility is uplifting to both man and woman. Do what needs to be done. Too often we aim too high, wanting to give our wives or husbands what we cannot even afford, so nothing ever happens, while basic necessities, everyday things that can get done for free, like partaking in some sexual intimacy, are neglected.

God gave us everything we need, having placed our fore-parents in a beautiful world and giving them beautiful naked bodies for them to be creative with. They were to engage their creative powers and unite to make things happen. And thus has mankind continued along this trend of creativity, as the whole world is now so populated with gadgets and all manner of things of man's imagination. Notwithstanding, his pursuit of material things has come to be his undoing, a distraction from focusing on what really matters, life and love. Husbands and wives lose interest in their love lives as the things of this world win control of their minds. Friends, television, work and other things seem to get the attention the spouse deserves.

By allowing ourselves to lose sight of the promises we have made, our relationships will grind to a halt and fail to reach the heights they otherwise would with undying devotion to our commitments. Disinterest fuels disinterest. Who wants to continue giving attention to someone who does not reciprocate it, or to someone who does not even deserve it? It is hard to treat someone like the majority when they treat you like a minority. We can aspire to higher heights in our relationships, but only if we are committed to loving, honoring and obeying – "If my people, who are called by my name, will humble themselves…" (2 Chronicles 7:14).

God is ever eager to bless us more abundantly than we could ever ask or think, but we are holding ourselves back from the fullness of His grace. Let your marriage be an opportunity for furthering your education in opening your heart to God's love through the opening of your life to another person. You have the right to choose, the right to withhold from God and lover, yet forego that right! Embrace the privilege of perpetual, inspired, intimate love.

CHAPTER 16

THE EVILS OF MONEY

Love is something that money cannot buy. Without money, however, it is difficult to maintain a happy home. Still, with or without money, a couple can lose focus on what is most important, focusing instead on material wealth. So there exists a great need in the world and in the church: balance in all things material and spiritual. Through the lifestyle of Christians, people may learn how to apply balance to their own lives. The world is watching, so the church ought to promote healthy living, even with special regard for the financial and the sexual aspects of life. Rather than criticize people for not living up to the Biblical standard, we are to demonstrate the importance of maintaining a wholesome way of life.

Creativity is key to living the kind of life others would wish to emulate. Couples must spend their money wisely and thoughtfully, maximizing the potential of every dollar and making the most of every cent. In like manner, couples must not merely interact for its own sake, but must make every moment with each other count. Just as money is to be well spent, time together must also be well spent. Being married is an opportunity to be as free in mind and body with each other as is a prostitute in the lewdness of her enterprise, so embrace the privilege!

Satan has a way of distorting the true value of things, and money and sex are no exception. Treating sex like a commodity that money can buy is one way in which the devil has caused it to achieve its now infamous 'taboo' status. But sex is beautiful…within the context God had meant for it: Marriage. Money is also a blessed tool…when used wisely, rather than 'loved' or used in pursuit of carnal pleasure. It is the work of darkness that brings about financial and sexual unease, as the two go very much hand in hand. Why, sex is the reason schools remain open! When you see the children playing in the schoolyard, you are seeing sex, because without it they would not be there. You are also seeing money, the money it takes to

> ## *"Treating sex like a commodity that money can buy is one way in which the devil has caused it to achieve its now infamous 'taboo' status."*

maintain their respective homes.

The first home was composed of only two people, but now there are over seven billion people in the world today! Through the many years that have passed, there have been wars, floods, famines and all kinds of catastrophes by which so many have died, yet the earth's population is maintained and continues to increase. The Lord God ever provides! Whether sexual or material, the riches of the earth are inexhaustible – God is good!

In spite of God's goodness, so much of the world's population is born outside of wedlock. This situation creates a less than ideal home for those involved, especially the children. More often than not, it is the father who is not around. With the absence of a parent generally comes a money shortage, making it that much more difficult to care for the fruits of the womb. So much needless pain could be averted through abstinence and other sexually responsible behaviors! But mankind ever insists on having its own way: fornication, adultery, one-night stands, rape…

When a man gets intimate with a woman once, sometimes he is not even aware of what has taken place – it means nothing to him. With some pregnancies, the men are not even certain they had entered the woman. It is only heard in the end that the woman is pregnant. Sometimes they are just mere girls, and they become ashamed; they go home to their mothers and are treated badly. Because of this experience, the girl may suffer emotional problems and not want to have sex ever again. If she gets married, this could be a problem in the marriage. Some of these girls are so naive that they do not even know what causes pregnancy. Why then should the man – many of them still boys in terms of their psychological development – take care of the child that he did not even want in the first place? Was it not just a little sex?

If people do not understand the 'ins' and 'outs' of this sensitive topic, how are they going to do better? If children are not shown the consequences of their actions from the beginning, parents along with everyone else of influence are just as irresponsible as the children are. Because humans are social beings, we are supposed to communicate wisdom to one another. Many have no one to talk to, and this is why the same mistakes are doggedly being made, generation after generation.

YOUR BEST COUNSELOR

There is a Supreme Counselor, Jesus Christ, the Perfect One. Nevertheless, we still need each other as fellow human beings, so from time to time we may ask the advice of someone we trust. When two people get married, many changes take place in their individual lives, and now they have each other. Two people become one. "Therefore shall a man leave his father and his mother, and shall cleave unto his wife: and they shall be one flesh" (Genesis 2:24).

The oneness meant for marriage is exceptionally unique! In this regard, many seem to not understand what this oneness entails. The bond of matrimony suggests that you cannot expect to make every decision on your own anymore; you cannot expect to live a private life anymore, nor can you expect to do things the way you used to do them, without consultation. To expect otherwise is to ignore a most vital part of who you have become. It cannot be business as usual. This is why your 'other half' should be your best counselor, your best confidant, your best everything. Once two persons openly express themselves and tell each other what their likes and dislikes are, there should be no pressing need for anyone else to advise such a couple regarding how to treat each other.

Caring partners know that little things need BIG attention. The microscope was developed for this very reason, allowing man to see the seemingly invisible. When couples have to seek advice from so-called

> *"When couples have to seek advice
> from so-called professionals,
> it is often because they have bypassed
> their best counselors,
> each other."*

professionals, it is often because they have bypassed their best counselors, each other. Wanting everything yet wanting to give little or nothing in return will cause couples to need more than a counselor. The disease of selfishness is not easy to live with, except for the one who has it. It can only be cured by the realization that love is real when it is freely given. Give love in abundance so that no earthly counselor will be needed. (Read 1 John 4)

CHAPTER 18

SELFISHNESS AND POVERTY

Selfishness has been with us from the moment sin entered the world. The devil is its originator, and it will continue to wreak havoc in our lives because we allow it to. If we were to eliminate selfishness from our lives, the world would be a better place. But Satan, that old serpent, has infiltrated the minds of men and women, often doing as he pleases with their lives. It is rather fortunate that Christ gives us a choice, the means through which we can choose goodness over evil.

Unselfishness, the opposite of selfishness, is the world's greatest blessing, yet the world plunges further and further into chaos because wrong choices abound and unselfishness is so rare. One who is selfish is numbered among the world's poorest (Luke 18:21-23), but there is good news: There are wise people who have lived, and there are still such people living in the world today. It is worth mentioning one who lived long ago…

Solomon, the wisest of them all, was called to rule Israel. The option was his to ask for whatever his heart desired. Solomon responded, Lord, give me wisdom that I might judge your people aright. Talk about unselfishness! Asking nothing for oneself does not necessarily make one poor.

Solomon ended up being the wisest, richest and greatest judge in Israel, as was demonstrated in his handling of the case of the two women and their babies (1 Kings 3).

Conversely, I could tell you about my grandfather who was rich and selfishly sold all he had, hoping for [strangers] to take care of him. He ended up in the poor house (infirmary) where he eventually died.

Man and woman were placed together by God to promote unselfishness. Despite this, marriage is where selfishness most commonly seems

> ## *"I could tell you about my grandfather who was rich and selfishly sold all he had, hoping for [strangers] to take care of him. He ended up in the poor house (infirmary) where he eventually died."*

to thrive. Two people cannot live together, have children together, live selfish lives together and then realistically expect their children to be unselfish. You could be setting your children up for the same poverty that you are living in. Henceforth, take a second look at the consequences of selfishness in contrast to the benefits of being unselfish.

Unselfishness is the reward of living a life free in Jesus, "doing unto others as you would have them do unto you." Such riches are not only for time, but also for eternity. Look to Jesus, the Giver of all good gifts, and you will never be poor. Jesus gave His life for the world (John 3:16); He made Himself poor that we might be rich. Accept His riches and selfishness will flee. I have tried it, and I love it! It is difficult to contain: I am happy for the liberation Jesus has given me! Would you also like to be free? Come along, join the celebration, and see the joy that salvation brings.

CHAPTER 19

THE WORLD IN ONE PERSON

The world is filled with so much variety – fruits, vegetables, trees, birds, fish, plants, animals, insects... God has made so many different species of living things. He alone is truly God! Of course, humans are not left out of the picture, as there are black men, white men, and all kinds of people in the world. And we all came from one couple: Adam and Eve! So what am I getting at – the world in one person? When you marry someone, you are essentially saying, "I don't need anybody else in my life. I'm happy enough with this one person," and you lock yourself away from everyone else ("…forsaking all others…"), though you still need people. In so doing, you become 'the world' to your wife or husband.

That is how it tends to be in the dawn of marriage, the early days of honeymoon excitement, when he cannot wait to see her to tell her how much he loves her. Then, as time goes by, he eventually stops saying it. By now she must know that he loves her, since he has put her in a big house and given her a king-sized bed. He also stops giving her flowers. They are the world to each other, after all. Soon thereafter, someone else starts doing the things long since taken for granted. It might even be enough to make her forget the big house, the king-sized bed and all the 'nice things'. Now husband and wife are both lonely, suffering silently in self-imposed prisons of mutual negligence.

"Spouses must always
seek to inspire the feeling
of having the world in each other
through the mutual bonds
of love and affection
that they both share."

It is the neglect of the not so "little things" that causes sex to feel like taboo. If the love is not sustained, both wife and husband are going to be jealous for something more. Spouses must always seek to inspire the feeling of having the world in each other through the mutual bonds of love and affection that they both share. Getting married does not mean that life is finished, for it has only just begun.

Fueling the fire of love is as much the wife's responsibility as it is the husband's. A husband wants to hear nice things too. I have heard it said, "Mi cook him food, mi clean him house – what more him want?" You have turned yourself into a maid without even knowing it. Be a wife! Rouse him to feel like you are the best woman in the world, especially after children.

A woman's figure changes for better or worse after pregnancy. It is to be expected, so do not respond negatively. Love changes the look of things. Live your lives for one another and the world will be yours…in each other.

DIVORCE

I recently saw the profile of a well-respected gentleman. He had listed his marital status as 'Divorced'. Divorce is not necessarily something we should be proud of; it is certainly not God's ideal for Christians, especially. Jesus said, "Whosoever shall put away his wife, except it be for fornication, and shall marry another, committeth adultery: and whoso marrieth her which is put away doth commit adultery" (Matthew 19:9). Strong words. I would like to reason with the Christian community on this matter.

Why do married Christian couples seem to take marriage as lightly as the rest of the world? Marriage should be taken so seriously that, even before one enters into it, one should purpose in his or her heart to make it work, with God's help. Too many marriages are built like a house of cards, held together by such things as finances and children. This is not ideal. Children are smart and they can tell when things are not going well between mom and dad. Put your spouse above your children, above everyone and everything else, and the children will get the love and security they really need.

When two people truly love each other, they will take better care of their family. In order to prevent divorce, you must love truly, which means putting God first and no longer living for self. If you need yourself so badly, you should never get married. Share your life. The joy of living must be in loving, sharing and giving. It can appear that you are doing your best while your beloved is doing nothing to make it work, but that is the devil's plan in action – while one works hard, he often tells the other to sit down. For this reason, it is vital for both of you to remember and practice the things that brought you together, so your marriage can be what God wants it to be.

God saw it was not good for the man to be alone, thus He made "an help meet (suitable) for him." Unfortunately, even the best gift can seem like the worst because of how we have allowed the devil to tamper with it.

"If you need yourself so badly, you should never get married."

It is really sad that we do not always live together in peace and harmony, for we cannot do without each other.

Husbands are killing wives, and wives are killing husbands. Let us be wary of the enemy behind all of this and get rid of him! One of the worst things that a couple can do to their children is to live badly with each other then end up divorcing. Good families are so few and the divorce rate is so high; the world is turned upside down, due to a breakdown in family life. Amidst the ensuing chaos, Satan is wroth because he knows he has but a short time.

I urge the world to give family life the respect it deserves. As humans, we may choose to live cheap lives, despite the reality that we are not cheap. We were bought with a price, the blood of Christ at Calvary. The only thing transferable from this world to the next is our good character procured by His blood. If we share this character with others, then we will be really living.

CHAPTER 21

THE LORD'S HERITAGE

Scripture declares that "children an heritage of the Lord" (Psalm 127:3). Children are great to have around! They are so relatively innocent and honest – children make families complete. Without our little ones, there would be no future; without them, the human race would become extinct within just about a hundred years. Children are needed for our survival as a species. No sex, no children; no sex, no survival.

God made a wonderful world, filled it with amazing creatures and gave them the gift of sexuality. As the Creator, He could have chosen another way of doing things, yet He did not. Though Satan attempts to make sex seem dirty, God has not changed His original plan of allowing sex to be the means by which life is perpetuated. Sex is not taboo, as Genesis 9:18,19 mentions the three sons of Noah through whom the whole earth was repopulated after the flood.

In the beginning, it was just two, Man and Woman, naked and unashamed. When God used animal skin to cover their nakedness, it was not because He was ashamed; it was man who had become ashamed as the direct result of sin. In Genesis 2:25 is seen the innocence of unashamedly accepting ourselves. God did not dictate what to do in sex, except to say, "Thou shalt not commit adultery" (Exodus 20:14). We ought not to be ashamed of our sexuality, neither should we run away from it. There is nothing negative about sex, as far as God is concerned. Sex is holy within the context of marriage, and the bed therein is undefiled.

The evil one has a counterfeit for everything that God blesses, so he confuses man about what to do and not to do. Prostitution, for instance, is one of the world's oldest professions. It just goes to show that even Satan does not have any hang-ups with sex and knows what he is doing. Unfortunately, Christians are often unaware of what is happening because we find it difficult to talk about sex, and the more we find it a difficult topic for discussion, the more our young people will have premarital sex.

*"When God used animal skin
to cover their nakedness,
it was not because He was ashamed;
it was man who had become ashamed
as the direct result of sin."*

I have made observations of women who talk openly about sex as opposed to those who do not. What I have noticed is that it is far more difficult to get the woman who talks about sex into bed than the one who does not. The apostle Paul was not married, yet he was able to write, "Let every man have his own wife, and let every woman have her own husband… The wife hath not power of her own body, but the husband: and likewise also the husband hath not power of his own body, but the wife. Defraud ye not one the other" (1 Corinthians 7:2-5). What God has blessed, let no one curse.

Take the taboo out of sex, live your life without guilt and put the devil to shame. We need to hear more sermons from the pulpit about sex, because it is an inseparable part of who we are; it is how we live and how the world continues, exactly as God had designed it. God's way is the best way, so let us try it His way and turn to His word (2 Timothy 3:16). If we live for Him, He will give us a better life. As we then train our children correctly, it will be great joy indeed to have them around and to see them mature into wise, responsible adults.

SEXUAL FREQUENCY

Sexual intercourse is not something to be rigidly scheduled. I believe lovemaking should involve a measure of spontaneity. Otherwise, is it really romance?

When you treat each other with respect and understanding and demonstrate genuine love, moments of intimacy may occur as many times as you desire, because true love engages both mind and body. But if you do not have that level of admiration and love for each other, once per month or even once per year could be too much. Who wants to live like that, anyway? Sensible couples, I am sure, want to experience the kind of harmony in which they are constantly bathed in the glow of genuine love demonstrated though consistent and sincere action. If you do to others what you would have them do to you, as the Bible directs, the odds of your having a good sex life will increase. It therefore means that if a couple starts finding sex boring, then something is terribly wrong!

There are warning signs… Is your relationship turning into a brother/sister connection? Do you see your husband as a yard-boy, or your wife as a maid? Do not allow any of this to happen! Whatever brought the two of you together should be preserved and improved upon. In turn, the question of how often will never arise.

Couples in love appreciate rabbit-like behavior. Ask "How often?" before you get married, not after you have been granted the license to drive.

"If ever the question of frequency becomes necessary, it may very well be time to call it quits, though the Bible does not sanction divorce in such cases."

Just drive carefully to avoid unnecessary accidents. The quality of a relationship can be determined by the 'quantity' question, for sex is not about pleasing oneself. If ever the question of frequency becomes necessary, it may very well be time to call it quits, though the Bible does not sanction divorce in such cases. The best thing, therefore, would be to continually strive to please your spouse. God simply wants us to find happiness in bringing happiness to others. It is not about how often. Do it when you can and it will keep you when you cannot.

CHAPTER 23

GRANTING FAVORS

No one really grants anybody favors in this life. Helping someone is a privilege granted to us, though we often do not realize it, as we like to beat our chests in celebration of our how good we think we are. There is none good, but God. We are here to serve one another, which is a gift from God, so should we not enjoy well doing in serving one another whenever possible? "For even the Son of man came not to be ministered unto, but to minister, and to give his life a ransom for many" (Mark 10:45). Since He, being our Lord and Master, is willing to serve us, He really, then, is the only one granting favors.

What we call favor is no favor at all, for without Christ we can do nothing. In Him we live and move and have our being. Because this book is about the human relationship in its highest state of being, the union of husband and wife, I ask, What have you done for your wife that you would call favor? Nothing, I hope. Otherwise, I am inclined to think you are a mad man. What have you done for your husband that you would call favor? Nothing, I hope. Otherwise, I am inclined to think you are a crazy woman.

We do things for ourselves all the time – do we then call it favor? We become ONE when we marry, yet I have heard husbands and wives saying, "A favor mi a grant him (or her)." I have been married for over thirty years and have never granted my wife a single favor. Marriage is commitment in action, a binding covenant; matrimony is a promissory tie that should never be broken. There are those of us who serve God as if we are granting Him a favor. Unfortunately, this attitude also invades our spousal relationships. It is wrong, humiliating and out of order. She is not your maid; he is not your gardener. Many marriages are failing simply because we fail to esteem one another according to Biblical standards.

'Paul speaks of "due benevolence" and esteeming others, even your spouse, more highly than yourself.'

Paul speaks of "due benevolence" and esteeming others, even your spouse, more highly than yourself. 1 Corinthians 7:3, 10:24 and Philippians 2:3 are golden rules. If followed, life will be as God intends. So let us not fool ourselves, for Satan knows what he is doing. He wants us to serve one another in the manner of his refusal to cooperate with God. He likes confrontation, and so he whispers to husbands, "Yu a big man! Nuh mek no woman tell yu what time fi come home at night..."; to wives he will say, "Don't mek no man harass yu fi sex! When yu feel like it, dat is time enough..."

The devil works in subtle ways, but as Jesus says, Even if it is your enemy who is hungry, feed him. We are not going to get to heaven by doing our own thing. Marriage is an institution designed to teach us and prepare us for what heaven is all about: He is coming back for a church adorned as a bride prepared for her husband. My wish is that all couples get the devil out of their lives, live beautifully and share this beauty with the world around them.

Why should we not talk about one of the greatest gifts that God has given to basically all living creatures? The packaged deal of physical pleasure and procreation, the marvel of His creative genius, inspires me to shout, "God is good!" God loves His creation, He Himself declaring it very good. Before sin, we lived like the animals, free as birds, naked and not ashamed.

But sin came and messed everything up. Sadly, we have accepted the shame rather than try to get rid of it. That is how dangerous sin is, though we all entered this world naked and without shame.

When a baby is born, it is the biggest talk in the family. Because of the love one has for the baby – even if one does not love or want the child –, a newborn is a topic of conversation. For better or worse, sex brings children into the world, and this will continue until Jesus comes. God knew exactly what he was doing when He made the entrance for sex the exit for babies.

Everybody talks about babies, so why not talk about sex? Young people who talk openly about these matters seldom get pregnant before they want to. They are smarter, more intelligent and more aware; they know where they come from and where they want to go. On the flipside, those who are 'shy' cannot talk about it, will not talk about it and do not talk about it. They are afraid of sex. Some are not even sure how they got here. They are attracted to the opposite sex and have normal feelings, but they do not talk about it. Instead, they 'end up' involved in what they were afraid to talk about: promiscuity, pregnancy and or disease. They do not know how or

> *"God knew exactly*
> *what he was doing when He made*
> *the entrance for sex the exit for babies... [Yet]*
> *Some are not even sure how they got here."*

why it happened, because they were not taught the intricacies of their sexuality.

Parents and guardians, I encourage you to educate your children in all things, even these. Sex education should begin as early as possible. Do not beat around the proverbial bush. Children are too precious! They are our joy and sometimes our sorrow, but love shines through it all. Accordingly, parents, pastors, educators, doctors, politicians and other persons with influence upon the lives of children and the wider society should speak openly with young people about sexuality. Believe me, it will not put them in trouble; rather, it will take them out. Do not allow the "If I only knew then what I know now" mantra to be the legacy you leave your children – this is why our world is so messed up! In the words of the apostle Paul, "Defraud ye not one another."

The marriage bed is undefiled, for it is honorable. God has no problem with sex. We humans are the ones with the sin problem. Satan has counterfeited every good thing that God has made; whatever God has blessed, Satan attempts to curse. But I can give God thanks for the Bible, the best book of all, which was able to liberate me from the devil's yoke of mental slavery that I was brought up under, where sex is concerned. Now I am as free as a bird: I am not afraid to talk about sex anymore!

CHAPTER 25

NO HOLDING BACK

Throughout their upbringing, most Christian children are repeatedly told to hold back from getting involved in sexual activities. When they have grown up and become of age, they are again told to save themselves for marriage. I suppose some will wait.

If you have (or will have) waited until you are married, why should you hold back once you have the 'license' for sexual freedom given by the Creator Himself? Those who have not waited let themselves loose long ago, so why should you be caged? It is the devil's plan to make good things look bad and bad things look good.

Satan has been a deceiver from the beginning, and he will continue to be for as long as we allow him. He even tricks the preacher into preaching temperance in a way that makes even married couples feel guilty for enjoying sex. Imagine this: A couple goes to church, the preacher preaches a good sermon, then they return home; one of them feels like kissing passionately, but the other says, "Remember that pastor said we must be temperate in all things." Understandably, one gets frustrated because the other is foolishly holding back because of a sermon. Now the devil laughs at them, since nothing like this ever happened when they were sweethearts. Next, he provides someone else to comfort the discomforted. That is how the enemy works! He is so cunning that most of us do not realize that he is the one working against us.

Amidst even the simplest of problems, if we are determined to live our lives free of condemnation, we need to be aware of how Satan works, in

"He even tricks the preacher into preaching temperance in a way that makes even married couples feel guilty for enjoying sex."

order to get him out of our homes and out of our lives. We must never allow Satan to deceive us with substitutes sent to fill the void created by a neglectful spouse.

Husbands and wives, no more negativity! Again, defraud ye not one another: the marriage bed is undefiled; marriage is honorable and so is sex within its holy boundaries. Be careful therefore, ministers, how you present your sermons on the subject, lest you confuse your congregations and lead them astray into mental slavery rather than guide them towards truth and freedom.

Surely, it is better for couples to live happily without feeling condemned in that which God says is good. Guilt and eventual divorce is precisely where Satan wants the Christian couple to end up, for he knows that most will want to marry again, which can complicate matters even further. Do not give him the satisfaction of destroying your marriage. Just as you enjoy good food, enjoy great sex with your spouse. Enjoy each other.

By the grace of God, let love flow unceasingly. Stop feeling guilty about God's blessings in your life. It is said that a hungry man is an angry man. Let there be no one angered as a result of sexual starvation in marriage, as well as no guilt associated with the desire to satisfy each other's hunger.

WHO IS THE GREATEST?

Who is the greatest? He who serves is the greatest. Sobering, yet how can this be? Is one not great if he is a doctor, lawyer, teacher, Prime Minister, President, or has lots of servants, money, women and land? Is she not great because of her good looks? The world defines greatness in material terms, and this is why it is in so much trouble. If we would look at greatness from Jesus' perspective, what a difference it would make! We are living, however, in a world where everybody wants to be boss.

The unending struggle for power and 'greatness' is not unique to any part of the world, and it affects Christians as well. Christian families ought to set an example for the rest of the world to follow, rather than yield to its influence. The family is the head of the world as Christ is the head of the [family].

When Jesus was here on earth, He served with distinction despite knowing it would eventually lead to the cross – real service. Imagine couples serving one another like they should… It would make a world of difference! Though it is sometimes hard to imagine serving others, it is a privilege when one gets the opportunity to serve. In serving, you might not always be shown appreciation for your service, but continue serving nonetheless, for such is the measure of true greatness. One of the reasons life is so hard is that many of us want everything without having to render any service for it. But the Bible assures us, "If ye be willing and obedient,

> ## *"Many people who are going through hard times in life are possibly reaping the fruit of selfishness."*

ye shall eat the good of the land" (Isaiah 1:19).

Our destiny is in our hands. Let us live a life of service to God and our fellowmen – this is really living. True service is doing what one does not necessarily like to do, or even want to, yet doing it willingly out of love. When you do only what you wish to do, there is neither challenge nor sacrifice. Love involves sacrificing what you love for someone or something that you love more. You do it for the happiness of the one(s) you love.

Jesus did not want to die, but He suffered the shame of the cross in order to save each and every one of us. It was not easy. He prayed, "If it be possible, let this cup pass from me," yet remained undeterred. Some of us, like Jesus, can love someone who does not love us, but let us be real. Persons in love will serve each other, and that is how they each become the greatest. Greatness comes with an unselfish attitude.

Many people who are going through hard times in life are possibly reaping the fruit of selfishness. Subsequently, I pray that couples will stop being selfish, start serving each other and thereby achieve true greatness.

Maybe we are afraid of giving good service for fear of being taken for granted. In such instances, remember Jesus. He came to serve us and we nailed Him to a cross. We spat on Him, in spite of His greatness! Jesus had never been equal with us, yet He "made himself of no reputation, and took upon himself the form of a servant, and was made in the likeness of men" (Philippians 2:7).

Heaven has gone to great lengths to help us change our sinful ways. That we follow God's precepts is heaven's core principle. Until such love fills our hearts, selfishness will continue to destroy any and everything. Rid your life of 'self' and you will see the change. If we would thus allow the Holy Spirit to lead our lives, we will make better couples, and better unions will improve our world.

CHAPTER 27

HOPE FOR MISMATCHED COUPLES

Who has the perfect dating method? I do not think anyone does. When a couple breaks up, there tends to be whispers that they did not spend enough time in getting to know each other. While that could be true, there are still others who will say the couple dated for too long. Long or short, a breakup is likely to occur if the relationship is not maintained.

There are couples that onlookers would describe as being mismatched, yet those very couples will have a fabulous life together. They somehow manage to defy the odds by remembering what the Bible teaches of Christ's dying for even the worst of us. This makes a huge difference and keeps the love of Jesus flowing throughout the course of the relationship – "Whoever comes to Me, I will not turn away."

When you are mismatched, it does not necessarily mean that love is not there. Some of us just do not know how to love. Rather, we are experts at walking away. If a person is willing to learn to love you better, show them how. If a person is not willing to learn, then that is the real problem, one transcending both short-term and long-term dating issues.

Relationships require knowledge of what love is and how best to care for it. Couples are like teachers who must learn these lessons from each other. What good teacher wants only bright students in their classroom? I certainly would not: I need a challenge! If one is willing to learn from me, I am worthy enough to teach them. Teachers who would teach only brilliant students are quite possibly lazy, maybe even dunces themselves. On the other hand, slow students are a crucible for producing better teachers.

When you can make the best out of a bad situation – that is how you

**"We want to live private,
insulated lives, even in marriage.
But it just does not
work like that."**

know you are a great teacher! Possibly the best partner you may ever have is the so-called 'mismatched' man or woman. Truth is, if the two who have entered their garden of love said "I love you" more often – not just saying it, but living it –, most couples would not bother to entertain thoughts of being mismatched. Even we ourselves as human beings are mismatched with the Savior of the world, yet He died for us all. Look at what He went through for loving us: He was treated like a common criminal, spat upon and crucified.

Unlike Christ, we do not want to experience any difficulty in life; we would rather not make any adjustments in our own lives. We want to live private, insulated lives, even in marriage. But it just does not work like that. If you want privacy, do not get married; if you do not want to share what you have, remain unmarried. If you are in love with yourself only, do not try to fool anyone, lest you fool yourself. People in a relationship must forget themselves. When that happens, each person will make the other feel important, then the inferiority complex will disappear.

Physical appearances can also cause some to feel mismatched, though sometimes it really is not an issue. Beyond the physical, there is something called ATTITUDE, which causes everything to go wrong when it is bad. The 'Beatitude' is the best attitude (Matthew 5:1-12); read and think about it. Perhaps it will change your attitude and help you realize you are not mismatched after all.

CHAPTER 28

WHATEVER IT TAKES

No one should ever become weary in well doing, especially not a husband or his wife. Your attitude towards the 'whatever it takes' concept may determine the success of your courtship and, ultimately, your marriage.

When a man finds a woman attractive and desires her, he will do whatever it takes to win her heart. Sure enough, if the woman is happy for his perseverance, she may fall for him. Early on in the relationship, however, most of the emotions are those of infatuation. In the longer term, the 'whatever it takes to win the woman's love' feeling can gradually turn into a 'whatever it takes to get rid of her' nightmare! This scenario can play itself out for either gender. Another hard fact of life.

Notwithstanding, if the words "whatever it takes" are more meaningfully applied by couples wanting their love to last, imagine how sweet and pleasant living with each other will be! But the same three words used merely as an empty promise can spiral into any sort of mayhem.

CHAPTER 29

GETTING SATAN OUT

We live in a world in which Satan is as much a reality as we humans are, with the exception that he cannot be seen. As a result, we are exposed to his wiles on a daily basis. He is ever present in our homes where his sole purpose is to destroy our marriages and our families. He seeks to destroy marriage because God has blessed it. So here is the question: How are we going to get him out of our homes when we cannot even see him?

Firstly, we must recognize the signs that indicate his presence: (1) when you are doing things that annoy your spouse yet do not care that you are hurting them; (2) when you are so in love with yourself that you forget your spouse; (3) when all you think about is "I" and what "I" needs; (4) when you want to stay married while still living a separate, private life; (5) when you do not want to be asked where you are… This sort of self-centeredness is a clear signal that Satan is thriving in your home and needs to GO.

Now is as good a time as any to put the devil out! Start with concern for each other's well being. This is a good way to demonstrate that God is in control of your home and your lives. Marriage is not as difficult as we

"Why should anyone want to hurt another? This can only be the work of the devil. Get him out of your house!"

make it out to be. All we need to do is remember that Satan is the destroyer of anything that is good.

The story is told of a man with a beautiful wife and a good job. After work, he would stop at the bar and drink until he got drunk. When he was asked why he kept drinking, his reply was that his wife "nah gwaan wid nuttin," and he was frustrated with her. As time went by, one of his drinking buddies told the wife what her husband had said and advised her on what to do to stop her husband from drinking. The advice was this: "When yu know yu husband near to come home, put on a sexy shorts and blouse, pretty up yu face and fix up yu hair. Spray on a nice perfume and meet him at the door, and a bet yu he will stop drinking!"

She decided to heed the advice. That first evening that her husband came home and saw her dressed up, he was speechless. When he finally regained his ability to speak, the drunkenness seemed to have instantly disappeared and he swore under his breath saying, "This is the kind of woman I have at home, and I'm staying out at bars drinking rum?"

Problem solved! From that day until now, all drinking has ceased. Satan does not want us to understand our spouses, so he distracts us and causes us to take each other for granted. Often without knowing it, we work along with the devil in doing negative things that can cause permanent damage.

The story of Samson and Delilah is a great example of the power of Satan's influence in relationships. Read Judges 14 and you will see how it can be when one spouse wants to destroy the other. Delilah manipulated Samson because she wanted to destroy him. She certainly knew how to show affection, so much so that Samson could not resist telling her his deepest secret, which she then used to bring him down.

God does not want us to destroy each other, but to support and build each other up. We should not want to tear each other down. If two have become one, the downfall of one is the pitfall of the other. Why should anyone want to hurt another? This can only be the work of the devil. Get him out of your house! Do not waste time living for worldly wealth alone; do not use each other for self-gratification. Put the devil to shame and he will flee from you, for God did not put you together to be unhappy – and even if you do not think God put you together, you can still ask Him to enter your life and allow Him to change you. The best relationships are not founded upon love at first sight, but upon learning to love each other through the process of time.

Our time on this earth is bound to expire, so why spend it in selfish misery? Allow God to take full control of your life, and live for each other. Only then can you really enjoy a full life together.

CHAPTER 30

A DISEASE CALLED LONELINESS

When someone is lonely, they rarely talk about it. Because we can be so insensitive to the needs of others, there are people who are practically dying from loneliness, even though they seem to have so much going on in their lives. Someone who commits suicide does not do it because they are happy or because everything is OK.

People like to pretend that everything is fine. But when something unfortunate happens, leaving us to wonder what might have caused it, it could very well be that the one who is most surprised is the very culprit that drove the suicide victim over the edge. This is why, oftentimes, there is so much crocodile tears shed at funerals.

It is therefore necessary that, as families and friends, we seek to do whatever it takes to promote happiness, joy and laughter among those with whom we are associated. Do not seek to destroy that which is good, but build on the good to make it better than best. There are good qualities in many of the persons around us, if we would only take the time to look.

Knowing our true potential, God wants to give us so much, which is why He sent His only Son to grant us access to the gift of eternal life. He promises us so much, even in this life, but we are often deprived because of our attitude toward others. Whether or not we receive some of the promised blessings is dependent on how we treat our fellow human beings – a

> ## *"Stand in front of the mirror and you might see...who the real culprit is."*

simple consequence of the Golden Rule. So if ever you are short on blessings, go stand in front of the mirror and you might see the one who is preventing you from receiving them. In time, the truth will set you free, as you discover who the real culprit is.

WHY SEX IS TABOO FOR SOME

Sexuality is a gift from God. As such, it should never be seen as or treated like taboo. Yet it remains the biggest taboo for some of us. Based on keen observation of people's behavior, I have realized that many of us do not know how to be affectionate with our spouses, and the only time some of us get close to them is when we want some action. We do not hug, kiss or say sweet and pleasant things to each other on a daily basis. No "Good morning, sweetheart," "Have a lovely day, my darling," or "How was your day, honey?" We neither say thanks for dinner nor for requests granted – nothing 'above' or 'beyond' comes from our lips.

We are a course set of lovers. And if this is how we are, how under God's heaven would sex not be seen as taboo? Some couples merely have intercourse and almost nothing else. So one can be married and still end up living an empty life. Can you imagine having a lover who wants nothing but sex from you? To the intelligent mind, THAT would be taboo, even boring!

A healthy love life consists of so much more than just the physical. Be romantic outside of the bedroom as well: call or message each other, say charming things throughout the day; try to be more creative as a couple and you will take the taboo out of sex. Your sex life will be more fulfilling, plus you will even have more of it! God wants us to be happy. Obey His words and your happiness is ultimately guaranteed.

CHAPTER 32

SHALLOW LOVE

The only type of love that some persons are capable of is the shallow, superficial kind. When selfishness hangs around, it translates into insensitivity, disrespectfulness, an unforgiving spirit and laziness, wanting all for oneself while giving little or nothing in return. But when love is deep, it yields the opposite, a more caring, giving and unselfish relationship. True love has depth and simply wants the best for others.

If someone is your sweetheart, why should shallow love exist when so much is at stake? If the land were dry and parched, would you try to prevent the raindrops from coming down? The type of love we are after is not an ordinary, holding-back kind of love; we want the real deal, romantic love. This is therefore all the more reason to acknowledge the distinction between the shallow and deep kinds of love.

There are those of us who confuse deep and shallow love as if they are not far apart, though in reality they are separated by great distance. Shallow love will make any relationship seem taboo, but deep love turns even negatives into positives. Deep love never grows weary in well doing; it does not tire. The only love that is deeper is God's love. The I AM, The Beginning and The Ending – He is everything. He is the greatest Lover of all, so let us try to love like Him. We cannot on our own, but He has promised to help us.

CHAPTER 33

REJECTION

No one ever chooses rejection. Getting rejected is painful and hurts deeply. Notwithstanding, our Creator and Redeemer came to earth and was spat upon was rejected. Can you imagine the shame? "He was wounded for our transgressions, he was bruised for our iniquities: the chastisement of our peace was upon him; and with his stripes we are healed" (Isaiah 53:5).

Being rejected did not take away our Lord's Creatorship or His Kingship, neither did it diminish the "I AM that I AM" in any way, shape or form. Fortunately, He knew who He was. He had a duty to perform, and He was not about to neglect that duty, whether with or without our love. Keeping the nature of His love for us in mind, do not ever think for a moment that you are of no value, even if you face rejection. There are times when the rejecter (or rejecters) does not know what is good for them – and even if they do know, they simply might not care.

The devil does not care about anyone. He wants us to be unhappy from rejection. With God's help, however, we can be made strong. I hope rejection is never a problem for you. If it is, pause, reflect, and be more thoughtful in your relations with others. The Bible is the book of books. Read it and you will discover the ultimate acceptance and grow in ways you never thought you could or would.

I have witnessed adversities, but with God's help they have made me stronger. I never knew I had so much resolve until the negative things of life reached me. As a matter of fact, this is what inspired me to put something on paper for the benefit of others, present and future. If I can help somebody, then my living will not have been in vain.

CHAPTER 34

STANDARD

In the beginning was God. He is the Creator. Our standard. He created the heaven and the earth. That is the standard. There is none beside Him. God is the only true God, the highest of all gods. This is why from the beginning He set a standard of righteousness that has no equal.

Lucifer could not deal with such high standards, so he rebelled against God's standard. With his low standard (which the world now accepts above God's standard), you can do any and everything and it is considered OK. How would you like to live in a world where anything goes? Answer this question with an honest heart. Personally, I would not like it. I would rather a country or world with better standards. Now, I am not saying that everything would be perfect, but having high standards does help to prevent the worst of calamities.

Having watched the news for years, I have seen many disasters that could have been avoided or minimized if higher standards were set. During an earthquake, for instance, some buildings fail because they were cheaply built to a very low standard, usually with very little steel or none at all, resulting in loss of lives. Yet some seem to prefer low standards, as the cheaper way is the easier way, and the dishonest way is the faster way. How sad! God knows the best way, therefore choose His way. We cannot have the best life if we choose the low standard. It may seem OK for a while, but remember there are consequences for our actions.

Whatever you decide to do, choose to do it with a high standard in

> *"It is the devil's plan*
> *to make high standards appear low*
> *and low standards appear elevated...*
> *Anything about marriage*
> *that appears negative did not come from God,*
> *but from the enemy."*

mind and for the right reasons. Always seek to do what is right, with respect to both yourself and others. The Lord God is a God of high standards and is ever watchful.

God made sex for us with the highest of standards in mind, although we humans seem to find this difficult to grasp, as our standards have fallen quite low. Even so, God gave us marriage, His greatest gift to mankind at creation, one woman for one man, saying, "Be fruitful, and multiply, and replenish the earth" (Genesis 1:28). Because of our low standards today, however, there are many for whom sex – God's amazing gift to humanity – is taboo. Unfortunately, this myth is found among Christians, as well. It is the devil's plan to make high standards appear low and low standards appear elevated. He was thrown out of heaven for this very reason. Married couples should therefore live a quality life, a life of high standards, because God is not pleased with low-class living. As Christians, we must be trendsetters. Anything about marriage that appears negative did not come from God, but from the enemy.

Satan wants people to be miserable, and he is certainly doing it very well. He is having a blast because some of us who are married allow him to have lots of fun while we experience the opposite. Misery, disappointments, heartaches, regrets – you name it. How much crazier can we get? Some are even miserable in the name of love, foolishly thinking that some physical and emotional abuse (beatings, withholding of affection) is to be expected in a healthy relationship. But this is contrary to God's plan.

Marriage must be a lifelong blessing for both parties. Everyday should be like a honeymoon. It may sound overly idealistic, but that is the kind of effort we should put into making it work – finding all this too idealistic is perhaps reason enough to seriously consider not getting married. Marriage is not for negative people, though many such folks are diving into it.

My standard is so high that I will never reach it, but at least I will always be climbing to a higher level. You too are invited to set high standards for yourself. Do not settle for mediocrity, for you are worth more than that. Look beyond the moon and reach for the stars. Having high standards is synonymous with achieving success.

As far as modern standards go, the U.S. Dollar has been the standard currency from since before I knew what money was. I have observed that their bills are of standard size and are all the same color. This makes sense. The dollar is the standard currency around the world, so it would not make much sense having all different colors, as that could cause a lot of confusion, especially since other currencies are multi-colored. So, in countless avenues of life, having a standard is important and sets you apart from the rest.

High standards are not primarily about what you want to get, but about what you want to give. It is about sharing, showing respect and standing for something to keep from falling for anything. By setting high standards for your marriage, your friendships and everything you are involved in, you will consistently seek to aim higher. Set high standards for yourself and your affairs. Our Creator is the God of the highest of standards. He invites us to reach toward Him. It is not always easy, but He will help us. Just take the first step and go for it!

CHAPTER 35

Energy has a very important role to play in any relationship. If one is in a relationship yet lacks the energy to carry out important duties, this could be a sign that something is very wrong. NASA sends many spacecrafts into space. Were there not enough energy to lift them off the ground, there would be no way to get those heavy objects into orbit. The amount of fuel and force it takes to push these crafts upward is tremendous!

As with a rocket ship, you need a lot of energy in a relationship to keep everything working well. A child who has lots of energy is always busy and cannot stay still. Do not allow your spouse to be so lacking in the energy department that all he or she wants to do is sleep. To get the best out of life, one must be energized. And who better to experience energy with than your spouse!

I know how it feels to be energized as well as to not be. When I am energized, the amount of things I get done in a day would possibly take days, weeks or even months otherwise. I have learnt from experience that some families struggle in life due to a lack of energy, yet couples do not even have to spend a cent for fuel to energize each other. Refueling starts right in the brain, and this energy encompasses so much more than just the sexual.

I have seen so many men and women put so much emphasis on sex that they forget there are other things that are just as important. I grew up in the countryside of Mount Pleasant, Hanover. Walking through the district, I will never forget hearing girls telling boys, "I have what it takes." I could not have been more than twelve years old – from that tender age, I have not forgotten. I realized even then that something is wrong with the way

"To get the best out of life, one must be energized."

we think. With such 'common' reasoning, we will never realize our full potential.

We must seek to love all we can, do all we can, give all we can, hug as much as we can, speak all the kindness we can, while being positive, wearing a smile instead of a frown, looking our best even at home, and always believing that we have done very little to deserve each other. In doing so, we will always want to do more. Learn to be appreciative of one another. If attention to seemingly small details is not the essence of real energy, I do not know what is. It is not costly. All you have to spend is time to think – thoughtfulness –, which means your brain will get some exercise. May we allow God to be our endless Source of energy.

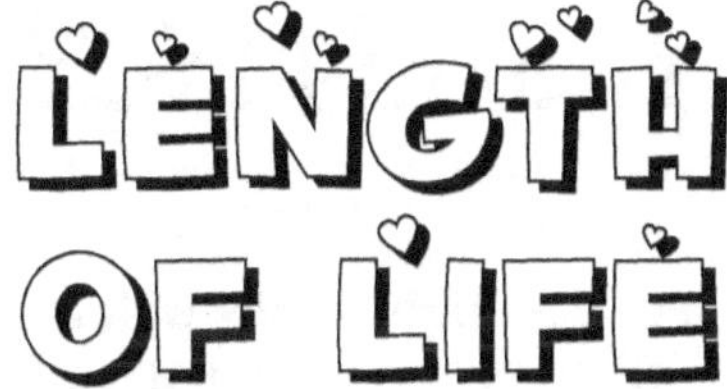

CHAPTER 36

LENGTH OF LIFE

No one knows for how long they are going to live. I believe most of us would like to live a long life, but, of course, without the aches and pains which so often accompany old age. Who would want to live forever with just one leg or one hand, or be bed-ridden for eternity? Can you imagine being basically helpless, with someone having to help you do everything, and you being consciously aware of all that is happening to you, how low you have been brought? These things can happen, and they do, in this sin-cursed world.

There are many harsh realities of this life that we human beings must inevitably face up to. Cruel as it is, death becomes a blessing. Therefore, make haste to live a good life. Waste no time in living like cats and dogs – we are much more valuable. God promises us eternal life. Claim it and you will receive it.

CHAPTER 37

MAINTAINING YOUR MARRIAGE

The preservation of marriage begins with both spouses not merely living with each other, but living for each other. We cannot do it on our own. We can try to for a while, but it will not last – if it does last, it is usually torture for the one who is actually trying. Only with God's help can we keep our desires under control. It is said that men think about sex much more than women do. How does a couple strike a balance in that equation?

Should you find yourself with someone whose libido exceeds your own, do not think of him or her as a sex maniac. Rather, reflect upon of how wonderfully God made woman for man and man for woman that your betrothed desires you more than food, which is the staff of life. It is a privilege for which you must be thankful; give thanks because God does all things well!

Whereas sex may well cause problems in some marriages, there would be no marriage without it. Accordingly, I encourage each one to purpose in their minds to do whatever it takes to enjoy sex and make their married life a happy one. Put away the negativity that festers in your mind and turns everything beautiful into a taboo. It is the devil's plan to keep people in darkness, for in him there is no light.

Let the light of Jesus guide you through the darkness of the evil one and put you on a hill from which your light may dispel further darkness. With the mind of Jesus in yours (Philippians 2:5), darkness disappears. Once you are in His light, you will be able to maintain your marriage to the maximum. May God bless your union! Amen.

CHAPTER 38

WAITING FOR THE OTHER WORLD

Most of us have been hearing about another world for a very long time. They say it is going to be a better world. I too have heard, and knowing about it makes me feel good – I believe it by faith. There are those of us, notwithstanding, who are so in love with the idea of that other world, and want to be there so badly, that we have no apparent use for this one. How smart is this?

This world is by sight, while the other world is by faith. Our senses, sight included, help us to have faith in that which we cannot see, hence my admonition that we live good lives in this present world as we, by faith, prepare for the one to come, which promises to be far more fulfilling. This world is a short-term one – just when you are getting ready to enjoy it, death says it is time to go. Yet before death finds us, the choice is ours to enjoy as much as we can, while we can, as often as we can, even as we await a better world.

Looking through the eyes of faith, we are assured that we can enjoy life as slowly as we want, as timely as we want, as relaxed as we want, knowing that time is not a factor in the coming world. But while we wait, let us not live in torment and be needlessly problematic to our fellowmen. One of the ways in which we can enjoy life here is in doing the things we will not be able to do when we are too old to do them. God gives us life: let us enjoy it to the fullest! Just remember that He can take it back whenever He is ready.

DECEPTION

No one likes being deceived, yet there seems to be so many deceivers around the world. Where do they come from? "Ye are of your father the devil, and the lusts of your father ye will do. He was a murderer from the beginning, and abode not in the truth, because there is no truth in him. When he speaketh a lie, he speaketh of his own: for he is a liar, and the father of it" (John 8:44).

We are fashioned after Satan's likeness, having been born in sin and shaped in iniquity. How can we, henceforth, thus put an end to deception? Accept Christ into your life and He will help you to be honest. Honesty is indeed the best policy. The many problems that confront us day after day can become things of the past, and the world a better place, if more would embrace an honest lifestyle.

Unfortunately, changing for the better is not always easy. There is deception in almost every area of our lives. In our schools, churches, banks and business places, deceptions are many. But deception in marriage is the most appalling of all, since the family is where society originates. If the head – or root, depending on how you look at it – is deceptive, it is all too easy for the offspring to continue the process.

Too many couples are getting together for the wrong reasons. In short, I say, STOP. The only right reason for marriage is love, genuine love. Love is not deceptive, because love is of God and God is love. Accept God's way and let deceptive practices become a thing of the past. Blessings from above are yet waiting to be bestowed.

CHAPTER 40

EXCITEMENT

Excitement seems to be one of the world's greatest cravings. People just want to have fun. And who should deny anyone that privilege? When a person is happy, it makes a huge difference in their life. As I penned this particular thought during the Berlin games of August 2009, there was a heightened level of excitement as the Jamaican athletes won so many medals that we could not have asked for anything more. Yet, as quickly as the games were finished, the merry-making also came to an end.

Unlike the wider world, some couples have no excitement in their relationship. It is a sad reality because this is where the world primarily needs excitement, considering that families form the basis of society. Excitement that is missing at home will be sought elsewhere, usually in the wrong places, which is always dangerous. And, indeed, there are many such places where one may find excitement: drugs, sex, sports, money, material things… But, truth is, this excitement that exists in the world is only for a time.

It behooves us therefore to choose the types of excitement that are beneficial to health, especially those that will live on even in the new world. God promises us a much better life, one so awesome that we cannot even begin to imagine what it will be like. Because we believe in the God of Creation, we look for His return, which will be most exciting for those who are waiting patiently for Him by faith. God is the God of excitement! Let us wait with heightened anticipation for that day when He will come again and receive us unto Himself, that where He is, there we may be also (John 14:1-3).

CHAPTER 41

WEDDING TRASH

A wedding ceremony is one of the most beautiful events one could ever attend. There is hardly any other function for which so much time is spent planning and preparing to ensure that everything is perfectly put together. A father will spend what he does not have, just to make sure his daughter is happy; a mother will go above and beyond for her son, especially if he is her only son. All well-wishers want to be involved in making the wedding the best it can be. So what could ever be trashy about a wedding?

It all too often seems that couples are more interested in having a splashy wedding – a competition to see which family can put on the best show – than they are in the quality of marriage they have after the rituals are over. If this does not make some weddings trash, I do not know what else does.

Imagine, we have allowed what God has made and blessed, something as beautiful as a man and a woman coming together in holy matrimony, to become of no value after the ceremony – taking into account the unfortunate experiences of numerous couples. We need to take a second look and ask ourselves why this is so. I will say this much: Satan is the author of trashiness; he is its cause.

Knowing the source of such ills, do not allow the devil to destroy your relationship. Let your married life be more meaningful than a mere wedding ceremony. Since you and I do not consider ourselves trash, we had better stop living lives that look like trash with God in it. It is more than possible: just let Him in!

CHAPTER 42

TAKING CARE OF YOUR YARD

There are countless stories of couples who do not take care of one another. These couples take each other for granted. Neither individual seems to realize that the degree of effort one puts out is either going to make or break the relationship. Yet both must carefully consider what they want. It is every couple's prerogative to consider this question: If outside affairs are more important than the home, why start a family?

The home should be considered the most valuable place, as it is where the next generation begins. Without good homes, the world will continue to be in chaos. We all seem to believe in disrespecting each other, though each of us wants to be respected. How selfish! The world needs quality families. Though it may seem impossible because of the evil one, you and I can start right where we are. We can even become examples for others.

Usain Bolt had to start somewhere on his way to becoming the world's fastest man who, in 2009, ran 9.58 seconds and 19.19 seconds in the 100 meter and 200 meter races, respectively. Like Bolt, we are all in training, but the One who coaches us is perfect. Our Heavenly Father is also more than willing to help us improve our relationships.

Many of us do not realize that the reason we disrespect others, especially our spouses, is that we do not respect ourselves like children of God should. An individual is seen as either ordinary or extraordinary based on the way they treat someone else. Nobody cares to settle with being ordinary; they would rather strive to become extraordinary. Therefore, be extraordinary, and take care of business in your own yard, lest you find yourself being ordinary and meddling in the less important affairs of others. God, the greatest Homebuilder, will help you. Try Him.

CHAPTER 43

WHO IS YOUR HERO?

Heroism is often associated with people who have done great things, such as fighting for some cause that benefits an institution, a country, a church, a school, a sports team, or saving someone's life from fire, drowning or some imminent danger. How fitting, then, that the accolade "hero" is worthy of such persons. Jamaica's world class athletes Usain Bolt, Asafa Powell, Shelly-Ann Fraser, Veronica Campbell, Melaine Walker and others are typical examples of athletic superstars we would call heroes. And there is nothing wrong with that. We should show our appreciation while people are still alive and able to receive it, hence the question: Who is your hero?

Above all, the Creator should be our first Hero. He died to save us from our sins and to give us a better life. Our second hero, as time would reveal, is that man or woman whom God gives us for a husband or wife. This gift should never be taken for granted. A husband should strive to be the best – and when he is the best, who then should be his wife's hero? Wives, stand by your man, live right, do well and be his best. Your husband should call no other his hero.

God made woman wonderful and oh so beautiful! Captivated by her beauty, Adam forgot to obey the greater Hero, the Creator, and instead ate of the fruit his wife gave him. As a result, the world is in grave distress today. If spouses expressed the level of excitement for each other that sports athletes and fans alike do for their favorite events, and keep God at the center of their enthusiasm, what a difference it would make in all our lives. We must aim to make our spouses our heroes.

CHAPTER 44

This book is not about making money – if it does, that is an added blessing. It exists primarily because I know that if I can help even one person to live a better life with his or her spouse, even after I am gone, then my life will have been worth living. I am one who likes justice. I like doing things to the best of my ability; I believe in giving my best, particularly when it comes to 'Man and Woman Story', especially as a man. I do not like the idea of folks crawling on their hands and knees begging me for anything, much more a woman. No, no, not for me! That is not my style; I do not feel empowered that way. That sort of thing might makes some men feel powerful, but it is not right. There is more power in humility than in any other so-called 'power'.

Jesus had access to supernatural power while here on earth, yet on numerous occasions He did not use it, so that we might live. He was so humble that a great many thought He could never be the Son of God. This is why I try to adopt a little of Jesus' humility by not allowing anyone to have to bow down to me for me to rise to the occasion.

As a man, I like to feel loved and wanted (as opposed to needed). I like surprises, and I like it when a woman is spontaneous. As a man, I like many things some women would think that men do not like. Just because it is never done for us or to us, or because we do not fuss about or talk about it, does not mean it does not matter to us. Think again, ladies!

As a man, I do not believe in enjoying a woman so much that I forget she wants to enjoy me too. What do I mean by this? Selfishness is a dangerous thing: it makes you unable to see anyone else's needs but your own. Imagine the woman in your life giving you her all, and you tell everybody how nice and sweet she is, while at the same time the poor woman is dying of loneliness, frustration and depression, all because of your one-

> ## *"As men, we are head of the greatest institution on earth, the family. Accordingly, let us rise to the occasion and do the right thing."*

sided relationship. This ought not to be. Men must be real men and do even the little things that women want to be done. If you do not know, ask, get help, change your style – more than likely the woman will respect and love you more. She will then be able to tell everyone how sweet, charming and wonderful you are, without telling a lie.

Men, we represent the King of the universe. Subsequently, woman is queen; therefore treat her as such. The role we have been given by God the Creator is wonderful, so we need to play it right. As men, we are head of the greatest institution on earth, the family. Accordingly, let us rise to the occasion and do the right thing. Worship would be deeper, fun would be more enjoyable, and life itself would be better – a foretaste of heaven on earth!

Ladies, if you are in agreement with the God-given role that men should play, go and do thou likewise. Faithfully fulfill your role of being queen to his king. I believe that by God's grace there can be peace in the home. May God bless your family!

CHAPTER 45

A USELESS DEVIL

Satan excels at helping us live miserable lives. He tells us to not do what we should be doing and to do that which we should not be doing. In this regard, that of conflict between right and wrong, the unmarried couples are not hypocrites; rather, the married couples living their lies are the biggest hypocrites. The world has few hypocrites, but the church has many.

Which would you say is more important – striving to keep a job, or learning how to keep a spouse? I have no greater joy than to see couples together and thriving, yet so many spend their time worrying about the world. Instead of worrying, simply trust and obey God and things will get better. Common sense is truly a rare commodity these days, but it is always available, and I heartily recommend we use it regularly.

One of the most sensible ways to survive is to not measure your progress against anyone else's, for God alone is our standard. If couples were to have even one percent of God's love for each other, it would be heaven on earth. If ten percent of the emphasis placed on earthly, material things were to be placed on our relationships, what a world it would be!

I am often jealous of dogs, cats, flowers, houses and such, because people spend so much of their time on these things. We must learn how to love and not merely tolerate each other. Herbert Edgar Douglas once noted that it is possible to have our heads filled with much information but little understanding. God tells us how to live and how to love Him through obedience. Satan, of course, wants to destroy us… Get him out of the picture and you and yours will be just fine.

CHAPTER 46

STIMULATING THE MIND

The mind is not something that you can see, yet one can read the mind. The mind is powerful, for it can make you and it can break you. This is why great care must be taken when two minds come together. Regarding the mind, the apostle Paul wrote, "Let this mind be in you which is also in Christ Jesus" (Philippians 2:5). The mind can be stimulated for good or evil, positive or negative. How, then, do you stimulate your spouse's mind?

When we encounter the word 'stimulate', we generally think of sex, something quite important to many of us. We must not forget, however, that mental stimulation is also essential for sexual stimulation to work right. Even the things we say can kill the mood or enhance it, make us want to work or take the day off. Though it cannot be seen, the mind is the most powerful sex organ in man and woman, an aspect of our being worth respecting.

Ladies, do not play with a man's mind. If you wish to play, be sure to play positively so you can reap positive results, or you might not like what you get. The flip of the script applies to us men, too. I often say that a woman who is sexy will get rid of a man who "nah gwaan wid nuttin" faster than a man would get rid of a woman who "nah seh nuttin." That being the case, ladies, you have a somewhat greater sexual role to play where the mind is concerned, because sex is more mental for you than it is for the man – you can fake it better than he can. A woman can more easily play games with a man's mind and then discard him as useless. God will hold such women guilty, especially if the man is blameless. The devil is remarkably experienced at using woman like Delilah and Jezebel to tempt man so that man's mind ends up scrambled and confused. As a result, many women hurt even themselves without even realizing it.

> *'I often say that a woman who is sexy will get rid of a man who "nah gwaan wid nuttin" faster than a man would get rid of a woman who "nah seh nuttin."'*

Thankfully, "Behind every successful man is a great woman." When a man is inspired by his lady's loveliness, the sky becomes the limit! While others may say your woman is not 'all that', you must do everything within your power to keep her radiant in all the ways that truly matter. We need to appreciate how the mind works and ask Jesus to lend us His mind so that our minds will always be positive. We use the power of our minds much too often to manipulate others for our own selfish purpose. If we were using it for each other, our families and societies, our world would be better.

Stimulating the mind is not a complicated venture. It is as simple as an "I love you," "I was thinking about you," "I miss you," and "What can I do for you?" Open the door for your woman, bring her a simple rose; cook your man's favorite meal, give him a surprise kiss... Whatever you do, let it be honest and meaningful always, the natural outpouring of a heart full of love.

THE HIDDEN MAN/WOMAN

In the beginning, God created man and woman. They were meant to live together in peace and harmony, but sin entered paradise and destroyed the tranquility that should have characterized the lives of the first two people God put together. Eve was not to leave the side of her husband, lest she be tempted. She wandered, and that was the beginning of the end of the perfect union between man and woman. Consequent to ensuing events, men and women today do not trust each other, even though they cannot do without each other.

These days, a man and a woman will meet for the first time, like what they see physically, and then make moves at each other. Unfortunately, they each have different agendas: the man is looking down the woman's blouse and up her skirt, while the woman is looking in the man's pocket. Because of their mutual superficial interests, neither bothers to ask the type of questions that foster a good relationship, for they are both selfish.

Because of selfishness, real love is hardly anywhere to be found nowadays. We want to be in a relationship, yet we hide our true self and deceive the one who is not smart enough to recognize our deception. But here is my advice: If you hope to find a good relationship, ask the man or woman any question that comes to mind – they will be happy to answer if they are sincere. This is how we learn, via questions and answers. When you hide who you are from the person you claim to love, you are simply setting yourself up for destruction later on in the relationship. If we each were to stop hiding ourselves from the one we plan to live with, it might take us longer to find the right partner, but it would be worth the wait. Never be so desperate that you attempt to use deception to get ahead in life… No! Honesty is always the best policy.

While is true that there are certain people in the world who get little or

> # *"Never be so desperate that you attempt to use deception to get ahead in life…"*

no respect because of their honest lifestyle, these are the people we should respect because at least we know who they are. They are like an open book: whoever knows them can read for themselves. How can you live with someone and yet be unable to figure him or her out? Such a lifestyle is unacceptable! I implore you to be honest and learn how to communicate. If you love someone, do not use them; they are not a pair of shoes, socks or underwear.

There is so much to enjoy in life, yet we deprive ourselves because of selfishness. If you love the one you are with, tell him or her – even if you do not, be honest still. When someone uses another, the abuser is no better than the prostitutes who sell themselves. So let us be vigilant and reveal the hidden man/woman.

1. Never assume.
2. Compliment more than you criticize.
3. It is OK to do things differently (i.e., there is more than one way to peel potatoes and fold the laundry…)
4. Always make time for the two of you.
5. Remember that the marriage begins after the wedding…
6. The best gift that you can give to your children is to love each other.
7. Be fair… Split the housework, spending money, and such, evenly.
8. Never go to bed angry.
9. Fight naked.
10. Agree to disagree.
11. Never ever mention the "D" word (divorce).
12. Do you want to be right or do you want to be married?
13. Always respect each other.
14. Do not be afraid to laugh at yourself.
15. Hang in there, because it is worth it!

16.   Love is not merely a feeling: it is a decision.
17.   Choose the one you love, and love the one you choose.
18.   Have a date night.
19.   Never pass up an opportunity to say, "I Love You."
20.   Hold hands.
21.   Marriage is not 50/50, but two people giving 100/100 all the time.
22.   Hug and kiss everyday, several times a day.
23.   Be quick to say, "I'm sorry."
24.   Always believe that you got better than you deserve.
25.   Never keep secrets from each other.

1. God made man as the crowning act of creation. We are more special than any other creature. (Genesis 1:27-31)
2. Sin has caused people to be ashamed of their nakedness; before sin there was no shame. (Genesis 3:8-11)
3. The three sons of Noah repopulated the whole earth, so sex could never be taboo in the sight of God. Why? Because He chose sex for procreation. (Genesis 9:19)
4. Sex is not only for procreation: it is a beautiful, pleasurable thing. (Genesis 12:11,12)
5. If love is not long-term, then it is not real. Love waits; love is persevering; love is kind; love is service. (Genesis 29:15-21)
6. When two get married, it is a binding covenant. You become a peculiar treasure to each other, above any other. That is how important the marriage relationship is. (Exodus 19:5)
7. A marriage is a sign between man and woman, just as the Sabbath is a sign between God and man. (Exodus 31:17)
8. A man should never lay with his daughter-in-law, neither a man with a man... (Leviticus 20:12,13)
9. Never allow your marriage to fall apart because you cannot have children. (1 Samuel 1:1-12)

10.   Lust is not love; love does not murder, and it does not harm.
      Read the story of David's lust for Uriah's wife... (2 Samuel 2)
11.   Couples must be wise: your future is in your hands.
      (Proverbs 6:6-8)
12.   If you do not take care of your spouse, somebody else
      might just do it for you. (Proverbs 7:16-23)
13.   It is important to make your bedroom special, so that
      no stranger will entice you. (Proverbs 8:11)
14.   Wisdom is from God. Be wise. (Proverbs 9:10)
15.   Ladies, do not be too clamorous, lest you end up
      being foolish (Proverbs 9:13)
16.   Do not make plans to cheat on your spouse;
      it may only be sweet for a while. (Proverbs 9:17,18)
17.   Appreciate instruction from one another. (Proverbs 12:1)
18.   Be the virtuous woman any sensible man would
      want to have around him. (Proverbs 12:4)
19.   Always be truthful. (Proverbs 12:22)
20.   Do not make your spouse's heart heavy,
      for it might stop. (Proverbs 12:25)
21.   Be the best at keeping each other's secrets. (Proverbs 13:3)
22.   Do not try to get rich too fast, or poverty might
      overtake you. (Poverty 13:7)
23.   Love instruction, for it can help you become rich. (Proverbs 13:18)
24.   Be the best parents you can be. Spare not the rod,
      lest you spoil your children. (Proverbs 13:24)
25.   There are times you are right yet you feel you are wrong,
      and times you might feel you are right even though you are wrong.
      Be careful. (Proverbs 14:12)
26.   Live right and you will improve your reputation. (Proverbs 14:34)
27.   Weigh your words before you speak. (Proverbs 15:1,2)
28.   Remember God is watching. (Proverbs 15:3)
29.   Little with God is better than plenty with Satan. (Proverbs 15:16,17)
30.   Folly is joy to him that is not wise. (Proverbs 15:21)
31.   Do not be greedy, as it could get you into trouble. (Proverbs 15:27)
32.   If you want to be honored, be humble. (Proverbs 15:33)
33.   Honey is sweet, but pleasant words are sweeter. (Proverbs 16:24)
34.   One who manages his/her anger is better than
      the mighty. (Proverbs 16:32)
35.   It is not the amount you have but what you do with what
      you have. (Proverbs 17:1)
36.   Do not be contentious. (Proverbs 17:14)
37.   Never stop being in love. (Proverbs 17:17)
38.   A merry heart does not attack: it is medicine. (Proverbs 17:22)

39. When one holds their peace, even if a fool, he or she is considered wise. (Proverbs 17:28)
40. A wounded spirit is difficult to bear. (Proverbs 18:14)
41. A good spouse is very special, a gift from God. (Proverb 18:22)
42. Even if you are poor, walk in integrity. (Proverbs 19:1)
43. Love your neighbors, even if they are poor. (Proverbs 19:4)
44. Wives, be prudent; you are from the Lord. (Proverbs 19:14)
45. Do not allow your children to deceive you. (Proverbs 20:11)
46. Do not be a trickster. (Proverbs 20:14)
47. Do not be a brawling woman. (Proverbs 21:9)
48. Open your arms to the poor. (Proverbs 21:13)
49. It is better to live outdoors than with an angry woman. (Proverbs 21:19)
50. God made and loves us all, rich and poor. (Proverbs 22:1,2)
51. Do not love to borrow: you might be someone's slave for a long time. (Proverbs 22:7)
52. Sow only what you desire to reap. (Proverbs 22:8)
53. Be generous to the poor. (Proverbs 22:9)
54. Take care of the less fortunate. (Proverbs 22:22)
55. Be faithful to each other. (Proverbs 25:19)
56. If your enemy is hungry, feed him. (Proverbs 25:21)
57. Rule your spirit. (Proverbs 25:28)
58. Never allow a fool to have more hope than you. (Proverbs 26:12)
59. Be a peaceful person, and do not make trouble. (Proverbs 26:21)
60. Be smart. (Proverbs 27:3)
61. Be open to hearing the truth; one does not lose when he is rebuked. (Proverbs 27:5)
62. Envy is dangerous: do not cherish it. (Proverbs 27:4)
63. Kisses do not necessarily mean love. (Proverbs 27:6)
64. When it rains heavily, ladies, weather the storm with him, rather than spring a leak. (Proverbs 27:15)
65. Women be careful of how much pressure you put on your husband for material gain. (Proverbs 28:20)
66. An evil eye will lead to poverty. (Proverbs 28:22)
67. Do not be too hasty in your words. (Proverbs 29:20)
68. Be as diligent and wise as the ant. (Proverbs 30:25)
69. Why did Solomon ask, "Who can find a virtuous woman?" My theory is that, although he had so many wives and concubines, he could not find love. Perhaps the women were going after him simply because of his riches and his fame. Very unfortunate. Real love should be the only reason that a man and a woman get together. Be virtuous in season and out of season. (Proverbs 31:10-13)

70.   No one should expect to get the best out of life without being
       willing to put in the effort. (Isaiah 1:19)
71.   No matter how in love you are, you cannot know a person's heart.
       (Jeremiah 17:9)
72.   Each of us is responsible for our own destiny. (Ezekiel 14:19,20)
73.   If relationships are to last, people must first purpose in their
       hearts to love unconditionally. (Daniel 1:8)
74.   We all have one Father, God our Creator.
       Let us live in peace. (Malachi 2:10)
75.   Love everyone, even the unlovable. (Matthew 5:46)
76.   Seek first to love the Provider before loving the things He provides.
       (Matthew 6:33)
77.   Love is simple, but selfishness makes it difficult. Whatever
       you would that your spouse should do for you, reciprocate.
       (Matthew 7:12)
78.   Do you want to be really great? Be a humble servant.
       (Matthew 20:26-28)
79.   If you want to achieve, prepare to endure. (Matthew 24:13)
80.   Real love forgets self. (Matthew 27:42)
81.   When one truly cares, little can become much. (Mark 4:8)
82.   Marriage is such a serious business! It makes me wonder
       why some Christians seem to take it so lightly. (Mark 10:2-12)
83.   The Bible has the answers for good living. Search the
       scriptures! (John 5:39)
84.   It is more blessed to give than receive. (Acts 20:35)
85.   Let no man seek his own, but every man another's wealth.
       (1 Corinthians 10:24)
86.   The word love, I believe, is the most used word in the world,
       but the least meant. (Read 1 Corinthians 13 over
       and over, and make love real in your life.)
87.   For one to be a great lover, one must be able to spread joy.
       Because this fundamental ingredient tends to be in short supply,
       as my observations have revealed, some of those with whom I
       have spoken are merely tolerating each other. How sad!
       (Galatians 5:22)
88.   Husbands are told to love their wives as Christ loves the
       Church (Ephesians 5:25-31). This is serious business and
       must not be taken lightly. Just as the relationship between
       Christ and the Church is serious business, so too is marriage.
       If you want to enter the Kingdom you have to serve
       God with all your heart; likewise, if you want to have a
       good marriage.
89.   Would you like to have the mind of Christ? Ask Him to help you

and most of your problems will disappear. (Philippians 2:5)

90. The apostle Paul was not married, yet he was able to write, "Let every man have his own wife, and let every woman have her own husband… The wife hath not power of her own body, but the husband: and likewise also the husband hath not power of his own body, but the wife. Defraud ye not one the other" (1 Corinthians 7:2-5) – the words of an unmarried man who was inspired by the Holy Spirit to write about how husbands and wives should live. How interesting! These counsels were given to remind us that whoever is not prepared to live a life of unselfishness should not get married.

91. There is no fear in love (1 John 4:18,19). Love is nothing if it is not freely given away.

DOING WHAT SEEMS IMPOSSIBLE

As I converse with married couples throughout the years and hear stories that do not sound the way they should, I have told myself that I MUST try to do something about it. As a result, "Sex Is Not Taboo" was born. I believe that when people get married they should live lives representative of heaven right here on earth. Satan does not want us to be happy, and we allow him to steal our joy, unfortunately. If each person were to live an unselfish life, then all the world's sadness would turn to joy, and peace would reign.